GROW UP GRANDAD

GROW UP GRANDAD
by Gordon Steel

JOSEF WEINBERGER PLAYS

LONDON

Grow Up Grandad
First published in 2016
by Josef Weinberger Ltd
12-14 Mortimer Street, London W1T 3JJ
www.josef-weinberger.com / plays@jwmail.co.uk

ISBN: 978 0 85676 362 5

Printed by Short Run Press, Exeter

For Rebecca, more than words can say.

GROW UP GRANDAD was first presented by Steelworks Theatre Company at ARC, Stockton Arts Centre, Stockton on Tees on 3rd September 2015. The cast was as follows:

GRANDAD	Simon Truby
POPPY SENIOR	Liz Carney
POPPY JUNIOR	Eliza Dobson Rose Allen
MARGARET	Liz Carney
GENEVIVE	Liz Carney
MOLLY	Eliza Dobson Rose Allen

POPPY JUNIOR and MOLLY are played by the same actress. In the inaugural production Eliza Dobson and Rose Allen alternated performances.

Directed by Gordon Steel

Set Design by Alex Doidge-Green

Lighting Design by Alex Edwards

Costume Design by Gayle Playford

Stage Manager Sarah Edwards

Assistant Director Rebecca Steel

Original music by Andrew McIntyre

Assistant Stage Manager Emma Smith

CHARACTERS

GRANDAD

YOUNG POPPY, eleven years old

POPPY SENIOR, thirty two years old

MARGARET, POPPY'S aunt

GENEVIEVE, a social worker

MOLLY, POPPY SENIOR'S daughter

Note: Young Poppy is eleven when she first goes to live with Grandad but she is twelve when she leaves him and then we move on 20 years.

ACT ONE

Scene One

A woman enters DSL. She is in her early to mid-thirties and carries an old battered suitcase. She stands in a spotlight and thinks for a moment.

POPPY SENIOR (*sings*) *I'll never let you go, why because I love you.* If only it were true. I always thought it was . . . but today I'm . . . Grandads are happy jolly people aren't they? You know, freed from the constraints of parenthood and all the responsibility that entails, they are fun. They have fun. They like to have fun. They tell corny jokes (and think they're being funny, don't they?). They do silly little magic tricks, pull stupid faces. Slip you a bit of money and say, 'Don't tell your mother.' Not mine. He is the most awkward miserable tight-fisted bugger that's ever walked this planet. And he enjoys it. He enjoys being bloody awkward. He enjoys upsetting me. He enjoys upsetting anybody. He has the knack of making me feel so bloody inadequate and yet so bloody special. And I love his bones. But today, I am going to break his heart. I am going to do something I promised him I would never do. Oh God!

(*A man in his fifties enters from DSR and moves to DSC. He is wearing an overcoat, a cap and carries a newspaper which he proceeds to read. He is clearly unhappy.*)

Little did I know twenty years ago when he picked me up from school, it would come to this. I was such a happy carefree, naïve sweet little girl.

(Street noises and the noise of school children pouring out of school can be heard. POPPY, *an eleven year old schoolgirl in uniform enters, from DSR, backing on to the stage calling to someone off. She is pretty, but somewhat unkempt after a day at school: her school shirt hangs over her skirt and she carries a school bag.* POPPY SENIOR *exits.)*

POPPY Oh yeah, right-o. Like am bothered. Bothered! (*A beat.*) Yeah, you an' all. Aw go on . . . (*Pointing to her bum.*) kiss that. Kiss it, you knob-head. (*She turns right in front of* GRANDAD.) Grandad! (*A beat.*)

GRANDAD What did you call him?

POPPY (*a bit defensive*) A knob-head.

GRANDAD What sort of language is that?

POPPY What you doin' here?

GRANDAD I've come to pick you up.

POPPY Where's me mam?

GRANDAD Well she asked if I'd –

POPPY Me mam always picks me up. She wouldn't ask you to pick me up.

GRANDAD Well she bloody has.

POPPY But she doesn't even like ya'.

GRANDAD What?

POPPY And neither do I. In fact nobody likes ya'. Everybody thinks you're a –

GRANDAD (*curt*) Alright, alright calm down, you've made your point.

POPPY She said she was like just waiting for you to croak it!

GRANDAD Your mother said that!

(POPPY's *phone beeps, she has received a text. She checks the text.*)

POPPY Then we could have ya' money.

GRANDAD What money?

POPPY (*shouting across the street*) It's me Grandad!

GRANDAD What money?

POPPY Let's not like kid ourselves shall we, and that house must be like, worth a bit.

GRANDAD She's after my bloody house!

POPPY And the sooner the better she said.

GRANDAD Well you can tell her from me, I'm leaving it to a dog's home.

POPPY She said you would do that. She said, that, that like wicked (*Her phone beeps, she checks text.*) old . . . beep will probably like go and leave it to a beeping dog's home. You little . . . (*Shouting.*) Right Tit-head, I'm gonna knack you tomorrow.

GRANDAD What did you call him?

POPPY Who?

GRANDAD Him, him, that thing over there with the spots?

POPPY Tit-head. (*She sighs.*) Look Grandad, it's his name. Everyone calls him it. He's got these two little lumps on his forehead.

GRANDAD I don't care what he's got, you can't go round shouting things like that in the middle of the street.

POPPY But he called you a paedophile!

GRANDAD He did what!

POPPY (*showing him the phone*) A dirty Paedo, picking up little girls!

GRANDAD (*shouting*) Hey Tit-head, if I come over there I'll be with you.

POPPY Grandad!

GRANDAD (*shouting*) I'm gonna be telling your teacher of you.

POPPY Grandad!

GRANDAD You can't go round accusing people like that.

POPPY Calm down!

GRANDAD No bloody respect, some kids.

POPPY Look, Grandad, I can like get home on my own, I don't need you.

GRANDAD Well the thing is you aren't going home. You're coming home with me.

(*She snaps a look at* GRANDAD.)

POPPY I am not.

GRANDAD Your mam's asked if I would take you back to mine.

POPPY What's going on? You never like, pick me up. I never see you.

GRANDAD Well now's your chance.

POPPY Oh come on, the last time I saw you was like . . . Christmas day and that was a disaster.

GRANDAD Only 'cos you didn't wanna be there, you wouldn't even take your coat off.

POPPY Ya' didn't have the fire on! There must have been like six inches of snow outside and you didn't have the fire on.

GRANDAD And so you sat in the corner like a spoilt little girl.

POPPY Spoilt! I don't know how you dare. At least, I'm not like a bad-tempered, miserable old bas . . . beep! Who smells!

GRANDAD Smells?

POPPY Stinks.

GRANDAD I am bloody sure I don't stink.

POPPY I'm phoning me mam.

(*She takes her phone out of her pocket. He smells under his arms.*)

GRANDAD What are you doing?

POPPY I'm phoning me mam.

GRANDAD I forbid you to phone your mother.

(*She looks at him and defiantly starts dialling.*)

Put that phone away, now and we'll say no more about it. If you don't put that phone away I'll . . .

POPPY You'll what?

GRANDAD This is your mother's fault this, she's been too bloody soft with you. Stinks?

POPPY Come on.

GRANDAD I have a bath three times a week, I'll have you know.

POPPY It's gone to answering machine.

GRANDAD (*emphatically*) With Imperial Leather!

POPPY Mam, ring me as soon as you get this. Pond Life wants me to go to his house.

GRANDAD Pond Life?

POPPY I'm not going to your house.

GRANDAD Bloody Pond Life!

POPPY Look I'll go to Kelsey's.

GRANDAD No! Your mam asked me to pick you up. (*Trying to make amends.*) Look, let's not fall out shall we. Your mam wants you to come back to mine. It'll be dead exciting. There's no amount of fun we couldn't have. (*A brilliant idea.*) We could do a jigsaw puzzle!

POPPY Oh my God!

GRANDAD It's fifteen hundred pieces.

POPPY Grandad!

GRANDAD What?

POPPY I'm twelve.

GRANDAD (*a beat*) Is fifteen hundred pieces too many? I could get a smaller one. I could get one with eight hundred pieces, or even five hundred. Would five hundred pieces be better?

POPPY (*to the audience*) I don't believe this.

GRANDAD Oh come on, it'll be a fun few days.

POPPY (*shocked*) A few days!

GRANDAD I've got you some sweeties.

POPPY (*to the audience*) Oh my God, what is this man going on about?

GRANDAD Werthers Originals. Gorgeous. (*He smacks his lips.*)

POPPY Look, let me like, make this clear, I'm not going to your house for a few days, for a few hours, for a few minutes – end of!

GRANDAD (*a beat*) End of what?

POPPY What?

GRANDAD End of . . . what?

POPPY (*raising her voice*) Just end of. End of. I'm not going, end of. It's what people say.

GRANDAD Which people?

POPPY (*shouting*) Any bloody people!

GRANDAD Don't you raise your voice to me young lady and mind your language.

POPPY Oh my God!

GRANDAD Look I've had enough of this, come on.

(*He grabs her shoulder but she pulls away.*)

POPPY You lay one finger on me and I'm phoning Childline.

GRANDAD You can phone the man in the moon for all I care but you're coming home with me – end of.

POPPY Listen thicko, I'm – not – going.

GRANDAD Don't you bloody talk to me like that. (*He grabs her arm.*) Now bloody come on.

POPPY (*she wriggles free and starts shouting and generally putting on a performance*) Get off me. Gerrofff! Help! Help! Get off me you pervert!

(*The street noise increases as people begin to gather round.*)

GRANDAD What the hell are you doing?

POPPY Help me! Please someone help me. This man is trying to grab me.

GRANDAD Cut that out now. This isn't funny.

POPPY (*to the audience*) Loads of people started to gather round. It was quite exciting. (*Turning back to* GRANDAD.) I'm not going with you, you freak.

GRANDAD Poppy stop it!

POPPY (*to the audience*) I played to the crowd. I was always a bit of a drama queen. (*Turning to someone.*) This strange man is trying to take me away and I'm very scared.

GRANDAD (*to* POPPY) I'm warning you. Stop that, stop it now.

POPPY I don't want any sweets.

GRANDAD (*to the crowd*) It's my granddaughter.

POPPY I don't want to see your puppies.

GRANDAD (*stupefied, he snaps a fierce look at* POPPY *before embarrassedly looking at the gathered group*) I never said that.

POPPY He did.

GRANDAD I never said that. (POPPY *nods.*) She's my granddaughter. No, no, no don't call the police, I can explain. Poppy will you tell this man who I am!

POPPY (*to the audience*) This man started to pull my Grandad away.

GRANDAD Who are you grabbing?

POPPY (*to the audience*) My Grandad hated anybody touching him.

GRANDAD Don't grab me!

POPPY (*to audience*) Grandad saw red.

GRANDAD Right come on then, if that's how you want to play it. (GRANDAD *starts to remove his coat and cap and throws them to the ground.*) But I'm warning you, Middlesbrough Junior Boxing champion!

POPPY (*to the audience*) Me mam said he made that up.

GRANDAD Three years running.

POPPY (*to the audience*) He wasn't.

(*He starts to bob and weave.*)

GRANDAD Come on then.

POPPY (*to the audience*) He thinks he's Mohammed Ali.

GRANDAD Come on then you big girl's blouse. (GRANDAD *starts sparring, throwing punches into the air.*) Come on then. Any time you like.

(GRANDAD *does an Ali-shuffle but feels a pull on the back of his thigh. But soon recovers and carries on, throwing punches.*)

POPPY Grandad! Grandad!

GRANDAD I'll knock seven kinds of shite out of . . . ya' what?

POPPY (*shouting*) Grandad, it's me teacher. It's me teacher! Grandad it's my teacher. And this is my Grandad. (GRANDAD *looks back and forward between* POPPY *and the teacher, as the penny drops, he forces out a whimpery laugh.* POPPY *talks to the audience.*) I got into so much trouble for that, I swear down, you wouldn't believe it. Grandad nearly punched Mr Dawkins. It made me dead popular in our class though. Grandad and Dawkins eventually kissed and made up.

GRANDAD No, no hard feelings. She can be a bit of a handful . . . (*He taps her on the back a few times, the last one somewhat forceful.*) can our Poppy.

POPPY Ow!

GRANDAD Oh yeah, I'll deal with her, don't you worry about that. Thanks for being so concerned. No, you did the right thing. (GRANDAD *laughs and then turns away.*) Dickhead.

POPPY You swore at my teacher.

GRANDAD He was lucky I didn't knock him out.

POPPY My mam says people who swear only do it because they don't have a good enough command of the English language.

GRANDAD Yeah well your mam's not here is she so she can –

POPPY Say it. Go on, say it. (*A beat.*) Your manner and your language is disgusting!

GRANDAD Mine!

POPPY Yours. (POPPY *takes her phone out and starts texting.*) Wait 'til I see me mam.

GRANDAD Wait 'til I see your mam.

POPPY Then you'll be for it.

GRANDAD I don't want to talk to you.

POPPY Oh grow up.

(*They set off walking.*)

POPPY What are you doing? You're not walking with me.

GRANDAD What?

POPPY I wouldn't dare walk down the street with you. Walk three steps behind me.

GRANDAD What?

POPPY I don't want people thinking I'm with you.

GRANDAD Who are you talking to, you?

POPPY You.

GRANDAD Well don't.

POPPY Or else?

GRANDAD You'll see.

POPPY Will I?

GRANDAD Yes.

Poppy (*pointing*) Three steps.

Grandad (*shouting*) An' I don't bloody stink!

Poppy Whatever.

Grandad Bloody Pond Life.

(*Fade to black out. Music, ten to fifteen seconds to segue into next scene.*)

Scene Two

Twenty minutes later. Poppy *enters her* Grandad's *house from a door S.L. The main living room is old and tired from years of neglect. It is littered with rubbish: old jigsaw boxes and puzzles, newspapers, half-empty plates of food and empty cups, books on sport and cricket, and a Middlesbrough Football Club scarf are scattered everywhere. A settee sits centre and an easy chair S.L. S.R. there is a fireplace, again strewn with clutter. A coffee table laden with books and papers sits on a worn rug in front of the settee.* Poppy *throws her school bag and coat on the floor and makes her way to a spot. During* Poppy's *address* Grandad *enters, gathers up her discarded belongings and tidies away the plates of half-eaten food and then sits in his armchair.*

Poppy I kept ringing me mam but there was no answer. His house was a tip and it stunk. It stunk like our downstairs cupboard of gas, old wellies and . . . cat pee. He'd always been a miserable old sod ever since I'd known him, but now he keeps looking at me and like trying to force out a smile.

(*He looks at her and tries to force out a smile.*)

Oh my good God, (*Her phone beeps as she receives a text.* Grandad *registers all the incoming texts: they become more annoying to him. She flops on a chair and checks it. Not looking up.*) This house is freezing.

Grandad: Well put your bloody coat on then.

Poppy: Can't you put the fire on?

Grandad: (*shocked*) In September?

Poppy: I'm cold.

Grandad: (*a beat*) Okay, yes, yes, I'll put the fire on, if that's what madam wants.

(*He switches the fire on.* Poppy *receives a text.*)

Poppy: (*to the audience*) I wasn't cold, I just did it to annoy him. (*To* Grandad.) Can't you turn it full on?

Grandad: (*aghast*) Full on?

Poppy: Yes.

Grandad: That fire's never been full on since we bought it. (*A beat.*) Right, bloody full on it is.

(Poppy *receives a text.*)

Poppy: (*patronising*) Thanks Grandad.

Grandad: It'll soon be warm in here. It'll be like toast in here before long. And then maybe we could turn it off again, you know, when we're sweating like pigs. (Poppy *receives another three text messages, one after the other.*) That's not going to annoy me at all.

POPPY What?

GRANDAD That thing there.

POPPY Me phone?

GRANDAD What the hell are you doing on it?

POPPY Nowt.

GRANDAD We'll you've been doing nowt for the last half hour. There's bloody bells going off in my head. Beep, beep, beep. You can't walk ten yards down the road without being glued to that bloody thing. Beep, beep, beep. Who the hell are you beep, beep, beeping?

POPPY Nobody.

GRANDAD Oh well that's alright then, that makes perfect sense. (*A beat.*) Is it Tit-head?

POPPY No it is not Tit-head thank you very much. If you must know I'm texting me mam, asking her to get me out of this bloody hell hole.

GRANDAD Watch your mouth.

POPPY Oh and you've got a mouth like a flower? Oh no! (*She shakes her phone.*) I don't believe it. It's died. (*A sudden realisation.*) I haven't got my charger. I don't suppose you've got a phone charger?

GRANDAD I haven't got a phone.

POPPY Oh God!

GRANDAD (*a beat*) I've got a land line, use that.

POPPY (*forceful*) I don't know her number.

GRANDAD (*forceful*) You've just been texting her.

POPPY But me phone's died. I can't get any numbers off my phone 'cos it's died. (*Pulls a face.*) Nnnn!

GRANDAD (*a beat, he chuckles*) Well that's a bit of a bugger isn't it? No more beep, beep bloody beep.

POPPY I was supposed to be dancing on a Monday.

GRANDAD Nobody told me that.

POPPY I told you.

GRANDAD When it was too late. We haven't got your dance gear have we?

POPPY And they're starting a new troupe. Ya' dunno what Miss Janine's like. She'll take it out on me.

GRANDAD Are you sure you don't fancy doing a –

POPPY Don't! Just don't mention a jigsaw. For crying out loud. Can I just say I don't want to do a jigsaw, I don't like doing jigsaws. I think jigsaws are boring. So don't ever mention doing a jigsaw again. Okay?

GRANDAD Okay. (*Pause.*) But if you change your mind.

POPPY (*raising her voice*) I won't change my mind!

GRANDAD Alright.

POPPY Right, if I'm not going dancing I might as well jump in the shower now.

GRANDAD That might be a bit awkward.

POPPY Why?

GRANDAD I haven't got a shower.

POPPY (*realising why he smells*) Oh well that explains it.

GRANDAD I do not stink. I've got a bath. I have a bath three times a week.

POPPY But I don't like baths. I like to shower.

GRANDAD You would do.

POPPY It's cleaner. It's more hygienic!

GRANDAD I've got this thing that you can stick over the tap, and that's like a shower. But you have to hold it in one hand and wash with the other so it might be a bit awkward. I've never bloody used it. No I tell a lie, I tried it once. But it was like showering with a live snake, I nearly bloody strangled myself with it. There was bloody water from here to hell and back. The bathroom was soaked. I flung the bloody thing in the garage, do you want me to get it?

POPPY Doesn't matter.

GRANDAD It's no trouble.

POPPY Forget it. Can I go on the computer?

GRANDAD I haven't got one.

POPPY You're jokin' aren't ya'!

GRANDAD No. I've got a telly.

POPPY (*she sighs*) Alright, I give up. Put the telly on.

GRANDAD I can't, it's broken.

POPPY You haven't got a telly?

GRANDAD Oh I've got one. There it is.

POPPY But it doesn't work.

GRANDAD Packed in last week. (*An idea.*) I know.

(GRANDAD *leaps up and exits.*)

POPPY (*to the audience*) This is blagging me head. The only thing he is interested in is like doing a bloody jigsaw. He does them and then he like glues them and hangs them all over the house like paintings. I can't stay here for a few days. I can't. What's he doing now?

(*He enters carrying an LP and a record player.*)

GRANDAD (*presenting*) Ta-dah.

POPPY What's that?

GRANDAD Found it last week in the garage. Me dad's old record player.

POPPY What are those?

Grandad Me dad's LPs.

Poppy What do they do?

Grandad What do they do? What do they do? They are records, albums, LPs.

Poppy (*the penny drops*) Oh, it's an old-fashioned CD.

Grandad No it is not an old-fashioned CD. It's not an old-fashioned anything. It's a record. I've got my record player here. A Dansette – they don't make 'em like this anymore. What music do you like?

Poppy Jessie J.

Grandad Jessie who?

Poppy The Vamps.

Grandad What about some Ronnie Hilton? You'll love this.

(*He takes the record out of its sleeve, blows on it, and searches round for his cloth.*)

Poppy Will I?

Grandad Your mam used to dance to this when she was little.

Poppy Did she?

Grandad She's always loved her music.

Poppy I can go on my phone, press a few buttons and get any music I like.

GRANDAD Not if you haven't got any charge you can't – end of.

POPPY It's not funny.

GRANDAD Where's me emery cloth? (*He cleans it meticulously with a specialised cleaning cloth, places it on the record player.*) I used to spend hours looking round record shops, trying to snap up a bargain. (*He lifts the arm and blows on the needle.*) Right here we go. (*He places it carefully on the record. It crackles and hisses.* POPPY *is unimpressed. The record plays at the wrong speed sounding a la Pinky and Perky.*) Oh bloody shit! (*He clicks something on the deck and the record reverts to its original speed.*) Wrong speed. (*He starts it again.*) Let's try again.

(*The record is 'Hey Look Me Over' by Ronnie Hilton.* GRANDAD *sings every word. He starts dancing across the room.* POPPY *covers her face in embarrassment.*)

POPPY Oh my God that's just wrong.

GRANDAD Come on you wanna dance. Let's dance.

POPPY I wouldn't dare. Grandad! Grandad! Oh my God!

(*He drags a reluctant* POPPY *on to the floor and dances her round the room. She eventually joins in, laughing and mocking* GRANDAD. *They have fun. Suddenly the record player explodes. They both turn, stupefied. Pause.*)

POPPY Oh shit!

GRANDAD Me Dansette De Luxe with automatic record changer.

POPPY Yeah, they don't make stuff like they used to do they?

GRANDAD Shurrup! (*With a sense of real loss.*) I loved that record player. It's a family heirloom is that.

POPPY I'm hungry.

GRANDAD Years I've had this record player.

POPPY I haven't had me tea.

GRANDAD I wonder where the manual is. I'll have it somewhere.

POPPY I've got to eat, God!

GRANDAD Right, let's take care of madam because madam is hungry. (*He sighs.*) Would you like a sandwich, I've got some chopped pork and ham, or a tin of Fray Bentos steak and kidney pie.

POPPY A . . . tin . . . of pie?

GRANDAD (*chuffed*) Fray Bentos.

POPPY A . . . tin . . . of pie?

GRANDAD Oh yeah, they're gorgeous.

POPPY I'm not eating a tin of pie.

GRANDAD Why not?

Poppy Because it's a tin of pie, and the thought of it makes me feel sick, that's why not. I want a McDonald's.

Grandad We are not eating that rubbish.

Poppy Oh, and like a pie in a tin is going to do me the world of good is it?

Grandad I can make that.

Poppy I'll have Shepherds Pie. I love Shepherds Pie.

Grandad I dunno how to make it.

Poppy (*sigh*) Lasagne then.

(Grandad *grimaces and shakes his head.*)

What can you make?

Grandad/ Poppy A tin of pie.

Poppy (*a beat*) Right, I'll have kids' food. I'll have chicken nuggets? Satisfied?

Grandad Right I'll go and get you some. That's not a problem. I'll nip to Tesco. Do you wanna come?

Poppy No.

(Grandad *goes to get his coat. Pauses. Contemplates for a moment.*)

Grandad I don't think I should leave you.

Poppy Why?

Grandad — There might be other stuff that you want.

Poppy — Look, I'm fine. I'm gonna stay here and kill meself. Just go.

Grandad — Right. (*He moves to exit and then checks. Pause.*) I can't go unless you come with me.

(Poppy *gets up and storms out.*)

Poppy — Right! Fine! I swear down, you're doing me head in.

Grandad — Wait there, I'll just get me bag for life.

(Grandad *gets his bag for life and follows* Poppy *out of the door. Music, eight to ten seconds link to next scene.*)

Scene Three

Lights. The next day.

Poppy — He burnt the chicken nuggets. Every single one of them. And the rest of the night was a disaster. I missed me mam. Grandad didn't notice. I didn't show him. I wasn't gonna let him know. But it was the first night I had ever spent away from my mam and I didn't like it. You know, when your mam's there you feel safe don't you? Going to bed was awful. I couldn't sleep. I tried squeezing my eyes shut and picturing me mam's face. The next few days were strange. When he picked me up from school, he gave me a big bag of sweets. I know. A big bag of Chocolate Butter Dainties. I'd never heard of 'em, but he seemed to think it was a big deal. He promised to get me a phone charger but he forgot. He took me to McDonald's, bless him. He asked for a cod tail end with mushy peas. I think he was just trying it on to prove a point. (GRANDAD *enters reading a letter.*) I could tell I was beginning to get on his nerves. He didn't know what to say to me. He kept hiding behind his newspaper.

(POPPY *sighs deeply and sits on the settee. She is bored.* GRANDAD *watches her. She looks at him and he pretends to read the newspaper. This sequence is repeated.*)

POPPY I'm bored.

GRANDAD Do you want to go and play on the swings?

POPPY Grandad, I'm twelve.

GRANDAD Oh, you never said. (*Exploding a little.*) I know you're bloody twelve. Every bloody time I suggest anything all you ever say is, 'Grandad, I'm twelve.' 'Grandad, I'm twelve'

POPPY It's not easy being twelve.

GRANDAD You're eleven.

POPPY I'm twelve.

GRANDAD When's your birthday?

POPPY 14th March.

GRANDAD What year?

POPPY (*pause*) Every year.

GRANDAD Oh hell.

POPPY Alright it's not easy being *nearly* twelve, 'cos ya' no longer a child and not quite an adult.

GRANDAD Don't be so ridiculous.

POPPY Well, what did you do when you were my age.

GRANDAD I was never bored I'll tell you that. I would do all sorts. I would climb trees, play tigs, football . . .

POPPY Right I'll go climb a tree and see how high I can get.

GRANDAD You will not, you might hurt yourself.

POPPY But you just said –

GRANDAD We were more sensible then. And it was a long time ago, we hadn't evolved as much, we were closer to monkeys.

POPPY What are you talking about? Can I go to the rink?

GRANDAD What?

POPPY The roller skating rink.

GRANDAD What for?

POPPY (*disgusted, shouts*) To roller skate!

GRANDAD In town?

POPPY Yeah.

GRANDAD Bugger off. It's like Beirut down there.

Poppy — But everyone else goes. All me mates'll be there and I'll be the only one left out. (*Bribing him.*) Me mam lets me go.

Grandad — Yeah, well your mam's not here.

Poppy — Oh come on Grandad. Can I go?

Grandad — No.

Poppy — I hate you.

Grandad — Good.

Poppy — (*she sighs*) Well what if you came with me.

Grandad — (*lowering the paper he is reading*) Roller-skating?

Poppy — You can watch from the café.

Grandad — Watch?

Poppy — You can enjoy yourself, complaining.

Grandad — Bloody watch.

Poppy — The cups are cracked and you get loads of froth in your coffee!

Grandad — I'm a doer not watcher. I've never watched in my life. Where's me coat?

(Grandad *exits.* Poppy *gets a pair of skates makes her way down stage and starts putting them on.*)

Poppy — And so we went roller skating. And guess what. (*A beat.*) Yeah, he wouldn't watch, he insisted on skating. (*She sighs.*) He couldn't even like, get the skates on. I mean I wasn't a brilliant skater, but when he got on the rink, oh my God, I swear down, he was like so embarrassing. And he was so nervous he kept . . . (*A beat.*) pumping. No, he did. And he wasn't subtle. Oh my God no. He just blasted it out. People were looking at him. I mean the man's got no shame. (*A beat.*) And it stunk. And then he said, 'Oh it's alright love, it's me tablets'. It was half an hour before he let go of the side.

(GRANDAD *enters unsteadily on skates.*)

GRANDAD (*as a train*) Choo, choo!

(*He looks decidedly uncomfortable but smiles bravely at* POPPY.)

This is fun isn't it?

POPPY Grandad, are you alright?

GRANDAD I'm grand.

POPPY Why don't you go and sit down?

GRANDAD I've just started.

POPPY You're embarrassing.

(*He falls and grabs on to* POPPY *who squeals and also nearly falls.*)

I told you to sit in the café. I'm gonna kill you.

(GRANDAD *starts to move round to the other side of* POPPY, *putting his hands all over her face and neck.*)

Get off me face you doyle. Ow, you're choking me. What are you doing?

(*The both stumble once more.*)

Come on, stand up for God's sake.

(*She helps him stand.*)

GRANDAD It's alright, I'm okay, I'm fine.

(*He stumbles and* POPPY *saves him again.*)

POPPY Right, let's get you back to the side. Come on, grab on to me. Are you on?

GRANDAD Yeah.

POPPY Are you sure?

GRANDAD Yeah.

POPPY Right-o, hang on tight. Come on let's go.

(*As they travel across the stage,* GRANDAD *farts.*)

GRANDAD (*rolling off-stage*) It's alright love it's me tablets.

POPPY Grandad you are disgusting. I don't believe you. (*To the audience.*) This young lad went zooming past and sent my Grandad spinning to the ground. (*Noise of* GRANDAD *falling and hitting the side from off-stage.*) Mind me, Grandad took it ever so well.

GRANDAD (*entering and calling off*) You big-nosed bugger

POPPY Are you alright Grandad?

GRANDAD Did you see what he did?

POPPY Have you hurt yourself?

GRANDAD Hey, you, you with the nose, come here. Yes you, Concorde.

VOICE (*off*) 'Sod off you daft old get!'

GRANDAD (*incensed, exiting in hot pursuit*) What! I was a boxer I'll have you know.

POPPY Grandad! Grandad! Don't! Leave him! (*To the audience while she takes off her skates and re-enters the house.*) Grandad was on one. I'd never seen him like that before. He told the boy to go away. Only he didn't say go away. He was like a man possessed, he like chased the lad through the reception area, and was just about to grab him when he tripped over the skates and ended up in agony on the floor. And the lad just stood there and laughed. Grandad was that mad, and tried to get up but couldn't. He was not happy!

(GRANDAD *enters through the door and stands. He has a face like thunder and his arm in a sling. Eventually* POPPY *plucks up the courage to ask him a question.*)

How's your arm?

GRANDAD Bloody hospital!

POPPY It was an accident.

GRANDAD Accident? Listen, I know people like that. One minute they're hanging round doorways and the next minute they're doing armed robberies.

POPPY Don't be ridiculous.

GRANDAD Is it? Is it? Is it ridiculous? Is it really? Let me tell you, little miss clever-clogs, before long that miscreant will be beating people over the head with a lead pipe.

POPPY He was only roller skating.

GRANDAD Criminals terrorising the streets and we do nothing about it.

POPPY We send them to jail.

GRANDAD Jail! Jail! Don't make me laugh. There was a judge the other week said it took a lot of courage to rob someone.

POPPY He did not.

GRANDAD He bloody did! A lot of courage to rob someone, You know what they should have done with him?

POPPY What?

GRANDAD Shot him.

POPPY You can't do that.

GRANDAD Over and done there and then. Bang, you're dead.

POPPY You can't just shoot him.

GRANDAD Why not? He didn't get there by accident. He didn't just take a wrong turn at the deli-counter in Tesco and then suddenly find himself in this guy's front room with a bag full of stolen gear, a shotgun in his hand and a balaclava over his head.

POPPY Grandad, They're not all murderers in jails.

GRANDAD Alright, for a lesser offence, make 'em work in the community, with uniforms on with little arrows on, so we know who the buggers are.

POPPY You might as well just go the, like, whole hog, and put them in the stocks.

GRANDAD I've got no problem with that. Putting 'em in stocks and then we could go round the back and kick their bloody arse. I'd be quite happy with that. I'd bloody love that. (*He mimes kicking someone.*) Get out you bugger! Oooh me bloody arm.

POPPY There's no talking to you. (POPPY *exits.*)

GRANDAD (*calling after her*) I'm telling you they should be taught a lesson.

POPPY (*off*) I'm not talking to you.

GRANDAD Come here, I've not finished with you yet.

(GRANDAD *exits in pursuit. F/BO music, ten seconds.*)

Scene Four

MARGARET *breezes into the room.* GRANDAD *follows.*

MARGARET (*taking in the room*) Oh dear!

GRANDAD What?

MARGARET (*patronising*) Well.

GRANDAD (*louder*) What?

MARGARET You've let this place go a bit, haven't you?

GRANDAD What's the matter with it?

MARGARET Look at it.

(GRANDAD *looks at it.*)

You said you were going to sort it.

GRANDAD Do you live here?

MARGARET No.

GRANDAD Well mind your own bloody business.

MARGARET Well look at it.

GRANDAD I do look at it. I look at it every day because I bloody live here. But that's not the point for God's sake. Where've you been 'til now?

MARGARET Oh I'm sorry I'm late, the plane was delayed.

GRANDAD Plane!

MARGARET It's much quicker than the train don't you think?

GRANDAD An aeroplane!

MARGARET Look, I'm busy, it was the only way I could fit it in.

Grandad — You came on a bloody sodding aeroplane to Middlesbrough?

Margaret — Don't start. I had a council meeting.

Grandad — Council meeting?

Margaret — (*casual and innocent*) Oh, didn't I mention it! They've just gone and elected me on to the Parish Council haven't they? I wasn't sure it was for me, but well, you know how it is when you're popular.

Grandad — Not really, no.

Margaret — I got here as soon as I could.

Grandad — It's taken you over a week.

Margaret — Alright, calm down. (*A beat.*) Where is she?

Grandad — Dancing.

Margaret — (*shocked*) Why aren't you there?

Grandad — Her mam's friend has taken her.

Margaret — You should be taking her. She needs you now. You can't be letting her go. Not at a time like this.

Grandad — Bugger off. I had enough of dancing with you and our Rose. Never again do I want to be in a room full of dance school mams, 'I can't believe our Bacardi and Coke came fourth, she won the All-England with that routine. I'm not having it. I'm not. I'm gonna have a word with that bloody judge.'

(Margaret *tidies up the settee before sitting on it.*)

MARGARET It wasn't that bad.

GRANDAD No it was worse.

MARGARET How's she doing?

GRANDAD How do you think she's doing? I'm constantly trying to keep her spirits up, make her laugh.

MARGARET Poor little mite.

GRANDAD (*pause*) Look, I dunno what to say to her.

MARGARET Well you wouldn't do, if you've been trying to cheer her up.

GRANDAD I even had to take her roller-skating.

MARGARET You did. It's a wonder you didn't end up in hospital.

GRANDAD She keeps asking questions. I keep fobbing her off and she knows I'm doing it. She's not stupid. She knows something's wrong. I don't know what to say to her. It's been over a week and I'm buggered. You know how long a week is. It's seven days! And seven nights. Seven long nights. The first night was murder. She never said anything but I could tell she was upset. I didn't know what to do, so I pretended I didn't notice.

MARGARET Poor thing!

GRANDAD Last night was the first time she's slept right through.

MARGARET Oh well, that's something anyway.

GRANDAD I slipped half an aspirin in her bed-time milk.

MARGARET You can't do that!

GRANDAD Never did you any harm.

MARGARET Look, we need to get this sorted and the sooner the better, because she can't live here.

GRANDAD I know.

MARGARET Not with you.

GRANDAD What?

MARGARET Well, you're terrible with kids.

GRANDAD What you talking about, I'm great with kids.

MARGARET Come on, when we were kids you told us that every time the ice cream van played his chimes it was because he'd run out of ice cream.

GRANDAD At least I've been there for her. (GRANDAD *stands.*) *I* can't just dip in on the moral high ground when I see fit.

MARGARET I hope you're not implying –

GRANDAD Look, we are the only family she's got. She's dependent on us. We have to do right by her.

MARGARET Of course.

GRANDAD And we have to tell her. It's getting ridiculous. So I thought we could do it tonight.

MARGARET Tonight!

GRANDAD Well we can't leave it any later. It's getting bloody impossible. And, to be honest, I'd prefer to do it with you here.

MARGARET (*pleasantly surprised*) Really?

GRANDAD Yeah. 'Cos I thought, perhaps, she could go an' live with you.

MARGARET Me!

GRANDAD It's just as easy feeding four as it is three. Just throw in a couple of extra potatoes.

MARGARET They're not bloody cattle.

GRANDAD And you've got four bloody huge bedrooms.

MARGARET And I've got three children who need their own space. It's important for their development. And what about Donald? Donald would be apoplectic at the thought of another child.

GRANDAD Bugger Donald?

MARGARET We budgeted for three. (*A beat.*) And besides with the private school they attend, they've . . .

GRANDAD What?

MARGARET Well they've been brought up differently.

GRANDAD You bloody snot.

MARGARET There's no need for that.

GRANDAD She's eleven years old.

MARGARET I'd like to help, I really would.

GRANDAD What you going to do, write a cheque?

MARGARET Yes, if it'll help.

GRANDAD She's a human being. You can't just buy her. You can't just pay her off.

MARGARET Look she can't come and live with me and that's the end of the matter.

GRANDAD Right, forget it. I'll sort it. You bugger off back to South Fork. I'll sort this out on my own.

MARGARET You're not capable.

GRANDAD Well I've done alright so far. We are getting on like a house on fire. She loves me.

(POPPY *comes bursting into the room.*)

POPPY You fat smelly pig.

MARGARET Really?

POPPY I told you didn't I?

GRANDAD Told me what?

POPPY But you wouldn't listen, (*Sarcastically.*) 'cos you know best. I'm gonna kill meself.

GRANDAD What?

POPPY No, I am, I'm not kidding.

GRANDAD What the hell have I done?

MARGARET What the hell have you done?

GRANDAD I don't know.

POPPY You wouldn't take me dancing.

GRANDAD You've just bloody been.

POPPY (*raising her voice*) Last Monday! Last Monday. I'm talking about last Monday!

MARGARET You should have taken her, I said that.

POPPY I've been thrown out of the troupe, haven't I!

GRANDAD Is that all?

POPPY No it's not all. I can't go to Blackpool.

MARGARET The All-England?

POPPY Yes.

MARGARET That's terrible.

GRANDAD Don't you start.

POPPY Kelsey's gonna be there an' everyone. I'll be the only one left out.

MARGARET You should have taken her.

GRANDAD I didn't know.

POPPY Aunty Margaret I hate it here.

MARGARET We all do darling.

POPPY He won't let me see me mam. Will you take me to her? She doesn't answer my calls or anything. Will you take me to her? Please Aunty Margaret. Please. I have to see her. I want to go home.

MARGARET Well . . . (*She looks to* GRANDAD *for support.*)

POPPY (*a thought*) He beats me.

GRANDAD/ MARGARET What!

POPPY He beats me, black and blue.

GRANDAD Don't start this game. Ignore her.

POPPY It's my own fault. I buttered his toast the wrong way.

GRANDAD What?

MARGARET Dad!

POPPY Do you want to see the bruises Aunty Margaret?

(*She starts to show some bruises.*)

GRANDAD That was the roller skating.

MARGARET What have you been doing to her?

GRANDAD (*aghast*) It was the roller skaing.

POPPY Don't hit me, please don't hit me.

GRANDAD I'll bloody hit you in a minute.

MARGARET You lay one finger on that little girl –

POPPY Will you take me to see my mam, Aunty Margaret, away from him. Please. Please, Aunty Margaret.

MARGARET Well . . .

POPPY I need to see her.

MARGARET It's not as easy as that.

POPPY Oh you're just as bad as him! Me mam was right about you, you fat bastard.

(*A short intake of breath!* MARGARET *is physically rocked by this attack.*)

MARGARET Don't you talk to me like that, I'm a Conservative councillor.

GRANDAD Conservative! You bastard!

(MARGARET *gropes for a seat, and cleans it with her handkerchief before sitting down.*)

POPPY (*losing it*) I hate living here. I want to see my mam. I'm sick of this smelly, filthy hell-hole. Where's me mam? Why won't anybody tell me what's going on?

(POPPY *starts throwing books and anything she can lay her hands on.*)

GRANDAD Stop that!

POPPY Where's me mam? Where is she? Tell me where she is.

GRANDAD I'm warning you.

POPPY Piss off Pond Life, you smelly bastard.

MARGARET Dad!

(MARGARET *shouts as* GRANDAD *slaps* POPPY'S *face. Silence.* GRANDAD *recoils.* POPPY *slowly stands and sobbing, stares at her* GRANDAD. *Upset, she walks out of the scene into a spotlight and talks to the audience.* GRANDAD *and* MARGARET *exit.*)

POPPY I don't think anybody had ever like hit me before. But how do you like tell someone that like . . . I felt sick. But like this might like sound strange, but I knew. Deep, deep down, I knew someat was up. She'd never not talked to me for a single day before. She wouldn't do that. We'd never spent a day apart. Grandad couldn't bring himself to say it and I didn't wanna hear it. But he did. He screamed it at me. Margaret went off it! She was like, well screaming and yelling. Grandad was shouting. I was crying. It was awful.

(GRANDAD *enters dressing in his black suit and tying his tie. Music – ten seconds.*)

POPPY Will you let me go to the funeral?

GRANDAD We've been through all this.

POPPY I know, but I wanna go. I wanna be there with me mam.

GRANDAD I would take you, honest, but I don't think it's a good idea. It'll only upset you.

POPPY It's my mam. It's not your mam. I have to go. I just have to go. I haven't said goodbye.

Please Grandad. You don't understand. The last time I saw her I wasn't talking to her. We fell out. It was before I went to school. I had these huge spots on me face and I covered them with a bit of make-up. Me mam went off it and wiped it off. So I wouldn't talk to her. She tried to kiss me and I wouldn't, she tried to cuddle me and I pushed her off 'cos I was annoyed. It was only a bit of foundation. And she always said that we should never part on bad terms. She would always make friends. Whenever I got into bed she would come in and kiss me and make friends and sing our song. (*She sings.*) *I'll never let you go . . .*

GRANDAD (*picks up the song*) *Why, because I love you?*

POPPY Do you know it?

GRANDAD Know it? That was your nana's favourite song. Her mam used to sing it to her and she would sing it to your mam.

POPPY If you never do anything else for me, just take me to say sorry.

(GRANDAD *walks.*)

POPPY Please Grandad.I'm begging you take to me see her.

GRANDAD I'm sorry, I really am.

(*He exits.*)

POPPY Grandad, please. (*Music – five seconds passage of time. To the audience.*) I hated him for it. How could he do that? I wouldn't speak to him. I was angry! I wanted to smash things up. I wanted to smash him up. I cried a lot. And what made it worse is that he . . . changed. He like, kept trying to cheer me up. He bought me a Crunchie every day. Me mam had died and he bought me a Crunchie. He said that as long as I was good I could have it, but I had to decide if I was good or not – so I always got it. But like, I suppose he was trying.

(*Lights.* GRANDAD *enters, proudly carrying a Shepherds Pie.*)

GRANDAD Ta-dah! I've made you . . . (*Proudly announcing his creation.*) a Shepherd's Pie.

POPPY I'm not hungry.

GRANDAD It's your favourite.

POPPY (*angrily*) I said I'm not hungry.

GRANDAD But you love Shepherds Pie. I've made it especially for you.

POPPY I don't want it.

GRANDAD I've put some brown sauce on.

POPPY (*raising her voice*) I said I don't want it!

(*She knocks it out of his hand on to the floor. A long pause. He looks at her and she defiantly glares back.* GRANDAD *acquiesces and starts to clean it up.*)

GRANDAD Look it's alright. It was an accident. These things happen. I'll soon have this lot cleaned up, don't you worry about that. I'm not really that hungry yet anyway. I bet it wasn't that nice. I'm not very good at making pies. Unless they're in a tin. (*He chuckles*, POPPY *is unamused.*) I'll put this in the bin and then I'll take you out for tea.

(GRANDAD *exits.* POPPY *sits on chair S.L.*)

POPPY (*to the audience*) I didn't see Aunty Margaret very much, she flew back to where she came from, but every now and again she would appear, and things would kick off. I would do things to annoy her and she would end up screaming at Grandad. Nothing he did was right. (*Music, five seconds passage of time.* GRANDAD *enters excitedly.*) He got it from all sides.

GRANDAD Oh you're there. Wait there.

(*He goes to exit again.*)

POPPY Margaret's been.

(*He stops dead in his tracks.*)

She's not happy.

(GRANDAD *turns to face* POPPY.)

Because I was ironing.

GRANDAD I've only been gone ten minutes.

POPPY She waited over an hour.

GRANDAD Oh God!

POPPY She said I was too young to be doing things like that.

GRANDAD You're twelve.

POPPY Eleven. But it was when I told her you called her Lady Shithouse that really made her flip.

GRANDAD What did you say that for?

POPPY So she'd really flip and oh my God did she go off it.

GRANDAD Oh for God's sake, Poppy! You're gonna get me into so much bloody trouble! Oh . . . I could bloody . . . Bloody hell! Wait there.

(*He exits.*)

POPPY What you doin'?

GRANDAD (*off*) Shurrup.

(GRANDAD *enters carrying the most enormous television.*)

POPPY What is it? What ya' doin? A new telly!

GRANDAD You don't deserve it!

POPPY It's massive.

GRANDAD I'm gonna take it back.

POPPY Grandad it's gonna be brilliant.

GRANDAD The man in the shop said, that I can watch cricket from morning until night.

POPPY Not if I've got the remote you can't.

GRANDAD And I've got a DVD machine to go with it as well. And a load of speakers. They're in the car. (*Proudly.*) It's a complete home movie system.

Poppy We can watch Dirty Dancing!

Grandad No we bloody well can't.

Poppy (*sings*) *Do you love me? Do you love me?*

(Poppy *teases and tries to dance with* Grandad *who seeks refuge behind the chair S.L.* Poppy *leaps on the chair, singing and teasing.*)

Grandad What are you doing?

Poppy *Do you love me? Do you love me?*

Grandad Bloody cut that out.

Poppy Come on let's get it set up.

(Poppy *starts to rip the tape off the box.*)

Grandad Woah, woah woah. Just wait right there. We need to read the manual first.

Poppy Just plug it in.

Grandad No one is going to touch that television until the instruction manual has been thoroughly and comprehensively digested. Until then, it stays in my bedroom.

(Grandad *exits with the television.*)

Poppy (*mimicking him*) Memememememememem. (Grandad *gives her a filthy look on the way out. To audience.*) It was two weeks before it got plugged in. He read the manual from cover to cover four times and he still didn't understand it. Eventually I couldn't take it anymore and waited until he went to the toilet and sorted it out. He loved it. He loved watching the cricket. He even put the fire on without being asked.

(*Music – Nostalgic ten seconds.* Poppy *sits in front of the fire.* Grandad *enters, walks to the fire and switches it on.* Poppy *looks at him and they both smile.* Grandad *sits in his armchair L, and switches on the television. A cricket commentary is heard.*)

Poppy — I went home today.

Grandad — What?

Poppy — It's up for sale. Our house is up for sale. I loved that house. You know when I think of . . . happy things, when I think of when I was happy, they're always in that house. Well they're certainly not in this house. (*A pause.*) I still miss her Grandad.

(A *long pause.* Grandad *is a little unsure how to respond. He switches off the television.*)

Grandad — We all do. (*A silence.*) But you're alright here aren't ya? We have a good time don't we? You've got everything you want haven't you? I'm doing my best aren't I? We have a laugh don't we, me and you?

(S*he turns to look at him. A pause.*)

I was thinking we could go to the beach.

Poppy — No thanks.

Grandad — Or we could go to the pictures.

(POPPY *trudges off.* GRANDAD *calls after her.*)

GRANDAD We could get a Chinese? (*Calling off.*) Shall we get a Chinese? Shall we put the home cinema on and blast the hell out of it? Let's watch Dirty Dancing. I'm gonna put Dirty Dancing on. (*He goes to put it on and realises he hasn't got a copy. He shouts upstairs.*) Have you got a copy?

(GRANDAD *is lost. He exits. Lights and Music – nostalgic ten seconds.*)

Scene Five

GRANDAD *enters with* GENEVIEVE, *a Social Worker.* GENEVIEVE *is a plain, hippy character, with a full-length flowery skirt, glasses, unkempt hair and quite overweight.*

GRANDAD Come in. Have a seat.

GENEVIEVE This place doesn't change does it?

(*She looks round the house. She can smell something.*)

GRANDAD Oh that bloody smell. It's the drains. Bloody council. I've got the decorators coming in, if you were wondering about the old décor. Yes, I'm getting it all done. Be as good as new. Would you like a cup of tea?

GENEVIEVE No, I'm fine, thanks.

GRANDAD I've got some cake.

GENEVIEVE No, I'm fine.

GRANDAD Bought it especially. Battenburg or Dundee?

GENEVIEVE No, really.

GRANDAD Watching your weight, I understand. (*A beat.*) Not that you need to watch your weight. 'Cos you don't. No, no, your weight's fine. You're just big boned. If anyone needs to watch their weight it's me. What a little fatty. (*He chuckles pathetically and changes the subject quickly.*) So Genevieve, it was nice of you to phone out of the blue like that.

GENEVIEVE Just wanted to call, see how you were getting on.

GRANDAD I can't remember the last time you popped round.

GENEVIEVE How's Poppy?

GRANDAD Oh she's great. Why?

GENEVIEVE I mean it must be hard for her.

GRANDAD It's hard for us all. Is this an official visit?

GENEVIEVE Oh no, no, no. It's just a social call. I was just thinking about you and thought I'd see how you were.

GRANDAD 'Cos you're a social worker aren't you Genevieve?

GENEVIEVE I was worried about you.

GRANDAD And you haven't got any kids.

GENEVIEVE No, I'm not married.

GRANDAD Oh that's right. I knew that. That's interesting isn't it? You know, you're job is talking about how best to bring children up and you don't have one. You've never done it. It's interesting that don't you think?

GENEVIEVE What?

GRANDAD I was just saying.

GENEVIEVE (*positive*) Her school says she's doing well.

GRANDAD Her school? You've been to the school.

GENEVIEVE I just happened to be in there on another matter and I asked how she was doing.

GRANDAD She never misses. I make sure of that. I know how important school is. I can't believe you've been to the school.

GENEVIEVE Yeah they said that. Margaret said that you'd have a few –

GRANDAD Margaret. Oh, of course. That's it. Margaret's put you up to this, hasn't she? She was home last week, to check up on us. She said she was gonna pop into the Council. It all fits in. Did you have a little chat, did you? Have a little chat over an Espresso choccy-woccy doo-dah and a cream cake? I bet you had a piece of cake then, didn't you?

GENEVIEVE Ken, please, there's no need –

GRANDAD You know. I have experience, bringing up children. Oh yes. I've done it before. Oh yeah not a problem. Just give 'em a good hiding now and again, keep 'em in check. Well, not literally give 'em a good hiding.

Genevieve Where is Poppy?

Grandad She's not in. She's out. Won't be back for hours.

Poppy (*off stage*) Ow! You little swine.

Grandad Although I could be mistaken. She must have come back early. You think she would have told me wouldn't you.

Genevieve I'd love to see her.

Grandad Would you?

Genevieve That's alright isn't it?

Grandad (*a beat*) Of course.

Genevieve (*calling very politely*) Poppy.

Poppy (*off*) What?

Grandad Could you come through for a minute please?

Poppy (*off*) I'm busy.

Grandad I need you sweetheart.

Poppy (*off*) What did you call me?

Grandad Could you come here please?

(Poppy *enters.*)

Poppy What did you call me?

Grandad Door!

(POPPY *moves back and slams the door.*)

(*laughing*) Kids eh? You remember Genevieve, don't you? She is a friend of your Aunty Margaret.

POPPY Really?

GRANDAD (*emphasising the importance of her title*) She's a Social Worker,

POPPY (*with enjoyment*) Is she now?

GENEVIEVE Hello Poppy?

POPPY (*sadly*) Have you come about Grandad's drink problem?

GENEVIEVE Sorry?

GRANDAD Don't start.

POPPY Oh! Me and my big mouth.

GRANDAD Poppy, darling. (*With a mean intensity.*) Cut it out. This is her idea of a little joke.

GENEVIEVE I'll tell you what Ken, I will have a cup of tea.

GRANDAD Will ya? Right. I'll go and put the kettle on. I'll probably put some washing in, maybe clean the windows, do a bit of polishing and ironing while I'm there. That's what I'm like you know. Always busy.

(*Once he is behind* GENEVIEVE, *he points threateningly at* POPPY *warning her to behave:* POPPY *smiles, taunting him.* GENEVIEVE *looks round and* GRANDAD *exits promptly.*)

GENEVIEVE I was talking to Mr. Dawkins yesterday, he said you were doing well in school.

POPPY Did he?

GENEVIEVE Do you like school?

POPPY It's alright.

GENEVIEVE What's your favourite lesson?

(POPPY *shrugs her shoulders.*)

Do you like P.E.?

(POPPY *shrugs her shoulders.*)

POPPY Never really do it. Never have any kit. Grandad never gets it washed.

(GRANDAD *opens the door.*)

GRANDAD You never tell me when it is.

POPPY Yes I do.

GRANDAD I'm not psychic.

POPPY I told you last week.

GRANDAD And I got it out.

POPPY It was soaking wet.

GRANDAD (*to* GENEVIEVE) We're having a bit of a problem with the dryer.

POPPY We haven't got one.

GRANDAD It's on order. (*To* GENEVIEVE.) Sorry.

(*He points accusingly at* POPPY, *then exits.*)

GENEVIEVE Do you like living here?

POPPY Oh yeah it's like Disneyland.

GRANDAD (*from behind the door*) I do me best.

GENEVIEVE Ken!

GRANDAD I'm not here. I've gone.

POPPY We haven't got a shower you know.

GENEVIEVE Really?

(GRANDAD *enters.*)

GRANDAD Sorry, I forgot to ask you, would you like a piece of cake?

GENEVIEVE You've already asked me. I'm fine.

GRANDAD Okay, fine, I'm out of here. Oh, and by the way if Poppy mentions a shower I mean she might not. She might not mention it all, but if she does, it's on order.

POPPY With the dryer?

GRANDAD It's important you look into it properly.

POPPY He's been looking into it for six months.

GRANDAD There's been a lot going on. And you can't rush these things, you can't be too careful these days.

POPPY So you've ordered a dryer and a shower.

GRANDAD Yes!

POPPY When?

GRANDAD Tomorrow. I'm ordering them tomorrow.

GENEVIEVE I'll tell you what, your Grandad's really busy. How about me taking you out for an ice cream?

POPPY Anything to get out of here.

GRANDAD No, I don't think that's a good idea, she has her homework to do.

POPPY What you talking about? I've done me homework, you've seen it.

GRANDAD Fine. Right, get your coat.

(POPPY *exits.*)

GENEVIEVE Oh, there was the incident at the school gates.

GRANDAD Incident?

GENEVIEVE Fighting?

GRANDAD Fighting. I'll kill her

GENEVIEVE No, no Poppy wasn't fighting. You were! With Mr. Dawkins.

GRANDAD (*the penny drops*) No no,no, that was just a little misunderstanding that's all. That was ages ago. And you think because of that. Oh my God!

(POPPY *enters.*)

POPPY Ready?

GRANDAD Right, have a nice time . . . sweetheart.

POPPY I will, don't you worry your little head on that score, honeybun. (*To* GENEVIEVE.) Can I call in the newsagents, I've run out of cigarettes.

(*She turns and smiles at* GRANDAD *as she exits.* GENEVIEVE *follows.* GRANDAD *thinks for a moment and then exits.*)

(POPPY *enters DSL and moves into a spotlight.*)

POPPY I was only having a bit of fun. I didn't mean it. It was a kind of game. I wish I hadn't now. I wish I'd just, like, you know, behaved, but it was decided that it was like best for everybody if I went to live somewhere else. They kept sending me on days out with happy smiley people who like gave me everything I wanted and kept buying me pink clothes. It did me head in. I didn't like 'em. It just felt . . . I dunno. But Cath and Brian were different. We got on. Do ya know what I mean? They were like . . . normal. We had a laugh, I'd never had a dad before and Brian was well . . . he was fun. And Cath, well she was like. . . well we got on. I could talk to her, tell her things. I had nights there and weekends away with them and then it was decided that I should like go and live there for a while, to see if I liked it. An' I don't know why, but I was dreading it. I liked 'em, I like 'em a lot, but . . . it's, I dunno, it's difficult to explain. I felt sorry for that miserable old . . . sod. He was gonna be all on his own. And I didn't like it. Grandad said he was dead excited and glad to see the back of me. I don't think he meant it. It was a strange day. He was sat in his chair as usual and . . . well I packed my case and dragged it downstairs.

(POPPY *exits. Music, ten seconds during segue to next scene.*)

Scene Six

GRANDAD *enters and listens, holding the door ajar.*

POPPY (*off*) It's alright Grandad, I can manage.

GRANDAD Good.

(GRANDAD *closes the door and quickly sits in his chair L, and pretends to read a newspaper.* POPPY *enters struggling with her suitcase. She is a bit lost.* GRANDAD *observes her. The instant she looks at him, he pretends to read. She sits on the settee and immediately stands again. She moves to the fireplace and runs her hand along it.*)

POPPY Cath'll be here soon.

GRANDAD She's outside in the car.

POPPY You can't leave her outside.

GRANDAD She wouldn't come in. She said . . . well . . . she said, she wanted me and you to have . . . she said there's no rush. Take as long as you want.

(A *beat.*)

POPPY Right.

(*She returns to the mantelpiece and checks herself in the mirror. All the time,* GRANDAD *is watching her. She turns.*)

Well there's no point hanging around is there?

GRANDAD What? Oh, right. (GRANDAD *gets out of the chair and throws the newspaper down.*) Well, I err . . . I guess not.

POPPY Right, I'll get going then.

GRANDAD Do you want anything to eat first? You can't go out on an empty stomach. Do you want a cup of tea or anything?

POPPY Since when have I drank tea?

GRANDAD Well milk, pop, anything? Do you want some pop? Do you want some milk?

POPPY No, I'm alight.

GRANDAD You have to have something.

POPPY Grandad, I'm fine.

GRANDAD Hot chocolate! I could make you some hot chocolate, would you like some hot chocolate?

POPPY Grandad, I'm fine. (*Reassuring him.*) I'm okay honest. Don't worry.

GRANDAD (*pause*) Oh, I forgot, I've got you a little something. Thought it might cheer you up. Close your eyes.

POPPY Grandad!

GRANDAD Close your eyes. Come on, close your eyes.

(*She sighs and closes her eyes.*)

Keep 'em closed. Right, put your hands out.

POPPY Grandad!

GRANDAD Put your hands out.

(*She puts her hands out.*)

Ta-dah.

(*He places a Crunchie in her hand.*)

POPPY A Crunchie!

GRANDAD Yeah.

POPPY A bloody Crunchie.

GRANDAD You like Crunchies.

POPPY It's you that bloody like's them.

GRANDAD (*a beat, a little hurt*) Yeah, but you like 'em an all don't you?

POPPY I'm leaving you to go and live with someone else and all you get me is a bloody sodding Crunchie.

GRANDAD It's a multi-pack to keep you going. And mind your language.

POPPY Well, you'd make a Saint swear.

GRANDAD I thought you were a lady.

POPPY I am a lady.

GRANDAD Well start behaving like one then.

POPPY Well I will when you start acting like a gentleman.

(A *pause*.)

GRANDAD You got everything?

POPPY I've got the photographs of me mam. But I don't think I'll keep that picture of you, it might give me nightmares.

GRANDAD Funny.

(*A pause*.)

POPPY Right, I'll best be off. Don't wanna keep her waiting, really.

GRANDAD No. (*A beat*.) No, it wouldn't do to keep her waiting.

POPPY No. No, that wouldn't do at all.

GRANDAD No it wouldn't.

POPPY Well, I guess this is it. I can get away from you and your moods.

GRANDAD Thank God.

POPPY Have a bit of freedom.

GRANDAD Give me a bit of peace.

POPPY We are gonna have such a good laugh.

GRANDAD I think I'll introduce myself to the remote.

POPPY It'll be loads of fun. And you don't get that here.

GRANDAD Hey, I'm a bloody good laugh.

POPPY When?

(*An awkward silence.*)

GRANDAD Look, you know I'm not one for making a fuss. You know for cuddling an' that. So well, have a good time.

(GRANDAD *proffers a handshake.*)

POPPY You wanna shake me hand?

GRANDAD That's what you do isn't it, when you're saying goodbye.

POPPY No it isn't.

GRANDAD Course it bloody is.

POPPY It is not. Now come here, you idiot.

(POPPY *brushes past it and flings herself at her* GRANDAD, *wrapping herself around him. It takes him by surprise.*)

GRANDAD Oh bloody hell.

(GRANDAD, *not used to such tactile treatment, stands with his arms out wide.*)

POPPY I don't wanna go.

(*Eventually he wraps his arms around her and pats her like a dog.*)

GRANDAD Hey, come on.

POPPY I'll tell you what. I'll just stay. I'll look after you. You can watch the cricket any time you like.

GRANDAD You're gonna have a bloody great time.

POPPY I'll tidy up me room. I'll do me homework. I'll eat tins of pie.

GRANDAD Hey, hey now, come on. Be a brave soldier.

POPPY I'm bloody twelve.

(*He tries to peel her off, but she grips on for all she's worth. Eventually* GRANDAD *succeeds.*)

GRANDAD You'll have loads of fun. Cath and Brian are dead excited about you. And you love them, you know you do. And I'll come and visit. And we'll go out.

POPPY Will we?

GRANDAD Yes, of course we will.

POPPY Promise me.

GRANDAD I promise.

POPPY You better.

GRANDAD I will.

(*Pause.*)

POPPY I'm sorry Grandad.

GRANDAD What for?

POPPY I've been a bit of a bugger haven't I?

GRANDAD Well . . .

POPPY I didn't mean it, you know.

GRANDAD I know.

POPPY I was just . . . well I was just . . .

GRANDAD You were just growing up, that's all. And now you've got that chance of a fresh start. You can go and show them how nice you are.

POPPY She's not me mam.

GRANDAD I know but in time –

POPPY No, not in time. Not never. She'll never be me mam.

GRANDAD I don't think she wants to be your mam. She just wants to . . . help.

POPPY And Brian he'll, well . . . he'll never be you.

GRANDAD Oh bloody hell.

POPPY (*a pause*) I'm gonna go now. (*Pause.*) Can I just say . . . (*A beat.*) . . . thanks for having me Grandad.

GRANDAD Oh don't say that, for God's sake.

POPPY I mean it. You're not the monster everyone says you are.

GRANDAD Thanks very much.

POPPY (*a pause*) Are you coming out to the car?

GRANDAD No. No. I'll not bother.

POPPY Right then.

GRANDAD I thought I might nip for a pint.

POPPY Can't you wait until I'm out of the house?

GRANDAD I was just saying.

POPPY Well don't. (POPPY *smiles.*) I'm gonna miss you Grandad.

(*She makes her way over to her case and picks it up. She checks, realises she has forgotten something, fishes in her pocket, and walks back to the coffee table.*)

POPPY Here is your front door key. I don't suppose I'll be needing it now.

(*She puts the key on the coffee table. She smiles at* GRANDAD, *turns, walks over to her case, picks it up, turns and makes her way out of the door.* GRANDAD *picks up the key.*)

GRANDAD Hey! (*She stops in the doorway and turns to look at him.*) Be good eh?

POPPY Don't you worry Grandad, I'll make you proud, don't you worry about that. (*A beat.*) Bye then fatty.

(*She exits quickly, dragging the case.* GRANDAD *is lost. He finds the remote, studies it. He presses it and the commentary from the Test Match can be heard. He sits and slowly crumbles. Lights fade to black out. Music. End of Act One.*)

ACT TWO

Scene One

We are now in a care home twenty years from now. It is minimalist: smart, modern and clean. The geography of the furniture mirrors the house of Act One. A bed sits where the settee used to be; Grandad's *chair L is now a modern high backed chair; and there is a set of sleek modern drawers R where the fireplace used to be. Adjacent to the door left, the telephone table is replaced with a small glass table that has a small vase with a flower in it.* Poppy Senior, *thirty two years old, enters carrying a large suitcase: the same suitcase that* Young Poppy *exited with at the end of Act One.* Poppy's *entrance mirrors Act One.*

Poppy S (*audience*) No, little did I know twenty years ago when he like picked me up from school what was in store. Little did I know it would like come to this. Life's cruel isn't it? (*Shouting.*) Come on.

Grandad (*off*) Shut up.

Poppy S (*shouting*) What are you doing?

Grandad (*off*) Bugger off.

(Grandad *enters, he has aged considerably: he is now an old man. He is unsteady on his feet and uses a walking stick. He stops and looks round the room somewhat confused.*)

Poppy S (*she lifts the case on to the bed*) This case weighs a ton. (*She starts to unpack some items.* Grandad, *confused, observes the room.*)

Grandad This isn't your house.

POPPY S — I know it's not.

GRANDAD — I thought it looked clean.

POPPY S — Funny. (*Sighs.*) *Look, w*e've been through all this, you're going on a little holiday.

GRANDAD — Holiday?

POPPY S — Yes.

GRANDAD — Where to?

POPPY S — Here!

GRANDAD — (*disgusted*) Here?

POPPY S — Yes.

GRANDAD — In Stockton?

POPPY S — They'll look after you here.

GRANDAD — I'm going on holiday to Stockton.

POPPY S — It'll do you good.

GRANDAD — I bet Scarborough's shitting itself.

POPPY S — Let me unpack your case.

GRANDAD — Don't bother.

POPPY S — It's no trouble.

(*She starts to unpack his case.*)

GRANDAD — No it isn't any trouble 'cos I'm not staying.

(*He goes to walk out,* POPPY *notices and quickly intercepts him.*)

POPPY S Hey where you going?

GRANDAD Home.

POPPY S Stop it. Stop being so bloody awkward.

POPPY S You can't stay on your own.

GRANDAD I've done alright so far.

POPPY S We've been through all this a million times, I found you asleep on the kitchen floor yesterday.

GRANDAD I was tired.

POPPY S And it's not the first time is it?

GRANDAD No, I've slept before, I do it every night.

POPPY S You'd fallen! And then I found you without any clothes on.

GRANDAD I was hot.

POPPY S You were in Tesco!

GRANDAD (*pause*) And what about Poppy? Who's going to look after Poppy? I can't leave her on her own.

(*He starts for the door.* POPPY S *checks him.*)

POPPY S I'm Poppy.

GRANDAD Don't be so bloody ridiculous. Poppy's twelve.

(*He starts to exit again.*)

Poppy S Poppy has grown up. Poppy is thirty two. And Poppy is me.

Grandad (*he studies her*) You?

Poppy S Yes Grandad.

Grandad You're Poppy.

Poppy S Yes.

Grandad (*a beat.*) 'Course you are. What am I saying? Eeeeh I'm crackers aren't I? You're Poppy?

Poppy S Yes.

Grandad My Poppy?

Poppy S Your Poppy.

Grandad Eeee, what's happened to me?

Poppy S Right lets get you sat down.

Grandad (*notices the case on the bed*) Am I going on holiday?

Poppy S Just for a few days.

Grandad Just for a few days!

Poppy S Yes. There ya' go.

Grandad What about Poppy? Who's going to look after Poppy?

Poppy S I'm Poppy.

GRANDAD Oh!

POPPY S Let me get you a glass of water.

GRANDAD Where are *you* gonna sleep?

POPPY S No, I'm not staying. I've got to get home, and get our Molly ready.

GRANDAD Molly! Molly's died.

POPPY S (*sighs*) Oh God! Yes, Molly, my nana, your wife, she's dead.

GRANDAD That's what I've just bloody said.

POPPY S But I have a daughter called Molly. Your great granddaughter, I named her after me nana.

GRANDAD (*a pause, he considers it*) It's confusing isn't it!

POPPY S It is confusing.

GRANDAD I don't know why you couldn't have bloody called her something else.

POPPY S I wish I bloody had now. Let's get your coat.

GRANDAD And you're leaving me here.

POPPY S Just for a couple of days.

GRANDAD On my own?

POPPY S There's people here can look after you.

GRANDAD I can look after meself.

POPPY S You'll meet new friends, there's loads of people here.

GRANDAD Where?

POPPY S We've just passed them.

GRANDAD Those old people gawping into space!

POPPY S They're not that old.

GRANDAD I think two of them were dead.

POPPY S This place comes highly recommended; they have all sorts of activities you can join in.

(POPPY S *takes a bunch of Crunchies out of his case. She smiles and places them on the drawers right.*)

GRANDAD Join in. Bloody join in. I don't wanna join in with anything thank you very much! If there's one thing I don't like doing it's joining in. Look I don't mind people enjoying themselves – as long as it doesn't involve me.

POPPY S What's this?

(*She has discovered a mobile phone tucked away in the lining of the case.*)

GRANDAD Oh that's mine.

POPPY S What are you doing with this?

GRANDAD Give it here.

POPPY S It's brand new.

GRANDAD Will you bloody give it here!

POPPY S It's like the one I used to have. I dropped it in the sink, can you remember? It broke me bloody heart. You said you were glad 'cos you were sick of seeing me on it.

GRANDAD Will you give me the bloody phone and stop poking round my things, and mind your own bloody business.

POPPY S Alright, alright.

GRANDAD I don't know why you can't keep your bloody nose out.

POPPY S Oh, I forgot, we have to pick your lunch.

GRANDAD I'm not hungry.

POPPY S You have a choice of roast pork, curry and rice or a quiche. What would you like?

GRANDAD Lasagne.

POPPY S Right, you can have the pork.

GRANDAD I like lasagne.

POPPY S But it's not on the menu.

GRANDAD (*mimicking her rhythm*) Well put it on the bloody menu.

POPPY S I'm just gonna nip through and hand this in and make sure they put a bit of arsenic in.

GRANDAD You'd like that wouldn't you.

POPPY S Yes.

(*She exits and* GRANDAD *sticks two fingers up. He looks down at the phone and smiles. Music – passage of time link, five seconds, flashback to happier days. Lose harsh modern light, with window gobos back to warmer home.*)

Scene Two

YOUNG POPPY *at eleven years old comes skipping in. He quickly squashes the phone down the side of the chair, concealing it from view. She takes a Crunchie off the drawers. The sound of Judge Judy emanates from the television.*

POPPY Grandad, Grandad.

GRANDAD Door!

(POPPY *closes the door forcibly.*)

POPPY I've had the best day I've ever had. You wanna see where they live. Oh my God! It's so much nicer than this dump.

GRANDAD It bloody would be.

POPPY No, Grandad, it is. It's clean.

GRANDAD This is bloody clean.

POPPY They have a cleaner.

GRANDAD We have a cleaner!

POPPY Who?

GRANDAD Me.

POPPY When?

Grandad I give this house a liberal spraying of Forest Pine every morning.

Poppy But their house, oh my God their house is like huge. Like off the telly huge. And you wanna see the bathroom.

Grandad I don't think I do really.

Poppy They have a telly in the bathroom. You can watch the telly in the bath.

Grandad But you don't like baths!

Poppy I do if you can watch the telly.

Grandad Well you'll not catch me washing my bits in front of Judge Judy, I'm telling you. (*He switches off the television.*)

Poppy And Brian, how funny is Brian. Oh my God, he's like, so funny.

Grandad Bit of a clown is he?

Poppy And like, Cath, wants me to go and stay for a weekend.

Grandad You didn't wanna go at all yesterday and now you're moving in.

Poppy I'm not moving in, I'm going for a weekend.

Grandad Right well we'll see, go and get ready for bed and then I've got a little surprise for you.

Poppy What is it?

Grandad Get ready for bed first.

Poppy Tell me.

Grandad Bed.

(*She runs to get changed, he feels for the phone. She checks.*)

Poppy Oh, I nearly forgot, you'll never guess what they've gone and bought me.

Grandad A small island in the Mediterranean.

Poppy (*amused by his suggestion*) No!

Grandad (*he flops his hand down*) Silly me!

Poppy What did I break on Friday night?

Grandad My will to live.

Poppy My phone, didn't I? I dropped it in the sink. Well they've just gone and bought me a new one haven't they?

Grandad Have they?

Poppy It's not just any phone

Grandad No it wouldn't be.

Poppy It's an iphone.

Grandad (*hiding his disappointment*) Is it?

Poppy An iphone 6-plus. Top of the range.

Grandad (*feigning a modicum of enthusiasm*) Oh well isn't that just bloody brilliant.

POPPY Yes it is. I can't wait to get to school, Kelsey will be like, green.

(POPPY *skips off excitedly.*)

GRANDAD Door!

(*Lights change back to the future.*)

Scene Three

POPPY SENIOR *bursts into the room and closes the door.*

POPPY S Alright calm down, I've closed it. Right, pork it is, with apple sauce. Christine's gonna be along later, to help you finish off the unpacking.

GRANDAD Christine?

POPPY S Yes, you've met her. You like her.

GRANDAD Christine?

POPPY S She's got all your tablets. You've got money haven't you?

GRANDAD I'm only on holiday aren't I?

POPPY S Yes, you're only on holiday.

GRANDAD It's just for a couple of days isn't it?

POPPY S That's right.

GRANDAD Then I can go home again.

POPPY S Then you can go home again.

GRANDAD That's good. I'm looking forward to going home again, now.

POPPY S Give it a chance. Don't be bloody awkward. Right give us a kiss, I'm going.

GRANDAD What?

POPPY S I'm late already and I've got stuff to do.

GRANDAD You're leaving me.

POPPY S I've told ya. I'm taking our Molly to Blackpool.

GRANDAD Blackpool?

POPPY S It's the All-England Championships.

GRANDAD I love Blackpool.

POPPY S Don't start.

GRANDAD We used to go every year with me mam and dad.

POPPY S Grandad, I'm gonna have to –

GRANDAD And when we got married I took Molly.

POPPY S You never said.

GRANDAD We stayed at . . . erm . . .

POPPY S Cherry Tree House?

GRANDAD That was it. Cherry Tree bloody House. Have you been?

POPPY S No, Grandad, look –

GRANDAD And me and Molly used to love walking down the Prom.

POPPY S Oh God!

GRANDAD Molly used to buy a kiss-me-quick hat. And a T-shirt that said –

POPPY S/ GRANDAD I'm with stupid.

GRANDAD Did I tell you the time I had fish and chips twice on the same night?

POPPY S Yes!

GRANDAD I had 'em early doors when we first went out. For me tea.

POPPY S And then you went to a show.

GRANDAD And then we went to a show.

POPPY S Was it Chubby Brown on the South Pier?

GRANDAD Chubby Brown on the South Pier.

POPPY S You never did.

GRANDAD Oh we did. Molly said she was disgusted –

GRANDAD/ POPPY S But she never stopped laughing.

POPPY S Look, Grandad, I'm really going to have to get going.

GRANDAD And we came out of the show and I said to Molly, I feel a bit peckish.

POPPY S And you had fish and chips again.

GRANDAD And I had fish and chips again.

POPPY S Oh good right, Listen –

GRANDAD Fish and chips twice in one night.

POPPY S . . . if you've forgotten anything, I'll bring it in next time I come. Right, give us a kiss.

GRANDAD Where you going?

POPPY S (*a beat, a little panicky*) Nowhere.

GRANDAD You're not going are you?

POPPY S No. Give us a kiss.

(*She kisses him tenderly.*)

GRANDAD I don't wanna stay here on me own. I don't like it.

POPPY S Please don't say that. Just try and enjoy it. You promised me. Look, you'll be getting your lunch soon.

GRANDAD Don't leave me here.

POPPY S Grandad, please.

GRANDAD Take me to Blackpool with you.

POPPY S Stop it.

GRANDAD I want some fish 'n chips.

POPPY S Please stop it.

GRANDAD I wanna go with you.

(*He grabs here wrist and holds it tight, she struggles to break free.*)

POPPY S — Ow, you're hurting me.

GRANDAD — I'll be no trouble.

POPPY S — Stop it!

GRANDAD — I'll pay for myself.

POPPY S — Do you think this is easy for me?

GRANDAD — I'll pay for everything.

POPPY S — I've never slept for bloody weeks.

GRANDAD — We can go and see a show.

POPPY S — You're doing this on purpose.

GRANDAD — I love going to Blackpool. You know I do. You know how much I love Blackpool. You're being selfish and nasty.

(POPPY S *breaks free.*)

POPPY S — Nasty! I don't know how you dare . . .

GRANDAD — Don't abandon me!

Poppy — Abandon you!

GRANDAD — I wanna go to Blackpool!

POPPY S — You bloody abandoned me more like.

GRANDAD — And see a show on the South Pier. We could go to the Tower.

POPPY S — I was a little girl. And I'm selfish! 'Cos where the hell's Margaret now? Come on. She got in touch with me so she wouldn't have to bother. (GRANDAD *starts to sing, 'Oh I do like to be beside the seaside . . .'*) I've dropped everything to come and look after you. And you're still having a go at me. You're still making me feel like shit. You ungrateful swine. I can't win. (*She runs out.*)

GRANDAD — (*singing*) . . . *Where the brass bands play tiddly om pom pom.* (*Pause.*) I love Blackpool.

(GRANDAD *smiles. Music in, Reginald Dixon playing the organ at the Tower Ballroom, Blackpool. Passage of time, five – ten seconds.*)

Scene Four

YOUNG POPPY *runs in excitedly and grabs her Crunchie as she speaks.*

POPPY — Grandad! Grandad!

GRANDAD — Door.

POPPY — (*sighs and closes the door*) You won't believe what has just happened to me. You'll never guess, you'll never guess.

GRANDAD — What?

POPPY — Well Guess!

GRANDAD — I don't know.

POPPY — Guess!

GRANDAD Right err . . . you went to Hartlepool and didn't get mugged.

POPPY No. Miss Janine has only like, gone and put me back in the troupe hasn't she?

GRANDAD (*forced excitement*) No!

POPPY Yes! She wants me in the troupe. I can't believe it. I can't believe it. And, you're not gonna believe this, wait for it . . . (*The big announcement.*) I can go to Blackpool for the North of England's. (*She screams.*)

GRANDAD Blackpool?

POPPY Yeah.

GRANDAD No!

POPPY Yeah.

GRANDAD I love Blackpool.

POPPY Don't start on that.

GRANDAD We used to go every year.

POPPY Grandad! I'm gonna smack you.

GRANDAD Me and Molly.

POPPY Grandad!

GRANDAD Walking down the prom.

POPPY GRANDAD! If you tell that story one more time. (*She dances and sings.*) *'I'm going, I'm going, yes, yes, I'm going'* .

(POPPY *takes a Crunchie off the drawers and starts eating it.*)

GRANDAD How're you gonna get there?

POPPY You're gonna take me on the coach, with everybody else's mam.

GRANDAD What?

POPPY Well what do you want me to do, swim it?

GRANDAD You are not seriously expecting me to go on a coach with a load of dance school mams.

POPPY Grow up Grandad.

GRANDAD Grow up! They wanna grow up. They're mad. They get away. They get on the vodka and limes. One thing leads to another. She said, you said this about my kid and before you know it all hell breaks loose and they're fighting like a couple of dogs.

POPPY Alight, calm down. God! Miss Janine knew you wouldn't wanna go, so she said she would look after me? And I get two days off school.

(*She picks her bag up and starts to exit.*)

GRANDAD Woah, woah, woah. Stop right there.

POPPY Don't start Grandad.

GRANDAD Two days off school!

POPPY Everybody else is.

GRANDAD Yeah, and that's why they're all bloody thick.

POPPY Kelsey's going.

GRANDAD Yes but Kelsey couldn't spell Bob backwards.

POPPY That's my friend you're talking about . . .

GRANDAD And she's thick. And so will you be if you start missing school.

POPPY But you wouldn't believe how nice Miss Janine has been with me. And we're getting all like new costumes. Brand new. She's had a mystery sponsor. I'm going, end of. I don't care what you say!

GRANDAD I'll think about it.

POPPY I have to go, please Grandad. I've done me homework; I'm doing well at school. I've been good, look. (*She holds up the Crunchie she's taken off the mantelpiece and dangles it in his face.*)

GRANDAD I'll think about it.

POPPY What makes you so bloody nasty?

GRANDAD I practice every night.

POPPY Ugh! Well I'm going, that's it. I don't care what you say.

(POPPY *exits.*)

GRANDAD Door.

(*She reappears in the doorway scowls at* GRANDAD *and slams the door shut.*)

Nobody puts Poppy in the corner.

(*He sits, looks round the room and thinks. He sighs. He picks up the phone, returns it to its box, gets his stick, stands and slowly makes his way over to the drawers. He puts the phone down and looks at the photograph of* YOUNG POPPY.)

Scene Five

POPPY *enters tentatively.*

POPPY Grandad!

GRANDAD Yes.

POPPY Is it, ya know, is it alright to well, you know, have feelings for somebody else?

GRANDAD Oh my God's she's got a boyfriend. Listen don't let him touch one hair of your body. What's his name? I'll talk to his parents. I forbid you to see him again. You're grounded. (*A beat.*) For two years.

POPPY It's not a boy. It's not about a boy. I don't like boys. I never have done and I never will.

GRANDAD Good, let's keep it that way. Filthy bloody animals they are. Can't trust a bloody word they say. They're only after one thing.

POPPY Grandad, it's not about boys. Calm yourself down. No, listen, this is important. it's just that well, me mam is me mam and well Cath's ever so nice to me, you know, we have chats an' that and well . . . I tell her things.

GRANDAD What kind of things?

POPPY Secrets.

GRANDAD Secrets!

POPPY You know.

GRANDAD No I don't bloody know.

POPPY Grandad.

GRANDAD What kind of bloody secrets?

POPPY The kind of secrets I wouldn't tell you.

GRANDAD What?

POPPY Well . . .

GRANDAD You've got secrets from me.

POPPY Well, you know . . .

GRANDAD I don't, bloody tell me.

POPPY You're . . . you're . . . well you're old-fashioned.

GRANDAD Old-fashioned!

POPPY You wouldn't understand.

GRANDAD Old-fashioned!

POPPY And I have to tell someone.

GRANDAD I'm bloody sure I'm not old-fashioned. The last thing I am, is old-fashioned. Tell me.

POPPY It doesn't matter.

GRANDAD No it does matter. You have to tell me now. You never keep secrets from your family.

POPPY Don't ya?

GRANDAD No, they are your family. You always tell your family everything. That's what they're there for.

POPPY Are you sure?

GRANDAD Yes!

(*Pause. She decides to continue.*)

POPPY Well it's like this, I talk to Cath and I feel guilty, because it isn't me mam. It's not right to talk to Cath when she isn't me mam, is it Grandad.

GRANDAD Oh God. Right. Well, it's like this . . . (*An idea.*) it's like having children. When you have your first, you love it with all your heart and you think you'll never be able to love anyone like that again. No one will ever take that baby's place. And then, you have another one, and you know, you love that baby every bit as much. You see every baby brings its own love. It doesn't mean you love the first one any less.

POPPY What are you talking about Grandad? I'm not pregnant. God!

GRANDAD That's enough of that kind of talk thank you very much.

POPPY You started it.

Grandad — All I'm trying to say, is that, your mam would want you to talk to Cath.

Poppy — Would she?

Grandad — Of course she would. You musn't bottle things up. It's better to talk about them and then they don't seem so bad.

Poppy — Do you think?

Grandad — Of course. Obviously I would prefer you to talk to me about them.

Poppy — Would you?

Grandad — But if you want to talk to Saint bloody Cathy Kirby, then do it. I'm not bothered. No, no, it doesn't bother me one bit. Do I look bothered? 'Cos I'm not.

Poppy — Alright Grandad. It's like this (*A beat, she takes a deep breath.*) I've started.

Grandad — (*pause*) What?

Poppy — You know. Started.

Grandad — (*pause*) Started!

Poppy — Yes.

Grandad — Started bloody what.

Poppy — Grandad . . .

Grandad — What?

Poppy — You know.

Grandad — I bloody don't know.

POPPY I've got my friend.

GRANDAD Kelsey?

POPPY I've got my period. Grandad, for crying out loud. I've got my period. My period!

GRANDAD (*unable to control himself*) Oh good God, don't say things like that. You shouldn't be saying things like that out loud. You're too young.

POPPY I'm a woman.

GRANDAD (*a beat*) How do you know? (*She looks at him knowingly.*) Oh yeah of course, oh my good God! I could kill your bloody mother for this.

POPPY It's alright Grandad. It's alright. Calm down. Cath and I have sorted it all out. It was only a little discharge in my knickers.

GRANDAD Woah, woah, woah! I don't bloody believe I'm hearing this. My God! Bloody hell! That's enough of that.

POPPY It's a very natural thing, it's all about –

GRANDAD (*puts his fingers in his ears*) Blah, Blah, blah, blah, blah blah. Molly, Molly why didn't I go first? When England take three wickets I have to have a lie down. But this. Get to your room.

POPPY What for?

GRANDAD Because I need to think.

POPPY What about?

GRANDAD Killing myself.

POPPY But Grandad, it's very –

GRANDAD Get to your room.

POPPY But –

GRANDAD Room. (POPPY *strops out of the room.*)

(GRANDAD *pours himself a whisky and drinks it. A ten second piece of music indicates a passage of time. The* SOCIAL WORKER *enters and sits on the chair left.*)

Scene Six

GRANDAD What the hell am I going to do?

GENEVIEVE I know she can be a handful, but so can all children. And you know Ken, we will give you all the support you need. We'll be there for you every step of the way.

GRANDAD I've never been one for touching and cuddling and you know . . . I can't give her all that nonsense. I mean, they love all that carry on, women, and it's not my thing.

GENEVIEVE But you've got children; you've done it all before.

GRANDAD No, that wasn't me. That was Molly. I was always working or drinking or playing sport or whatever. And you know, I always said to myself that if I had my time over again, I'd do it differently. I'd be there for my kids more, be there for Molly more. You know enjoy 'em more. Watch 'em grow up.

GENEVIEVE And now the opportunity's here.

GRANDAD Look the other week I walked into the bathroom, Poppy was there – with nothing on. She stood there and looked at me. She looked at me for a second or two and then pulled the towel in front of her. I don't think she even thought about it, it was just instinct. She pulled the towel in front of herself. I felt myself go red. I was beetroot. I didn't know what the hell to do with myself.

GENEVIEVE She's only twelve.

GRANDAD I bloody know how old she is. I apologised and left. I felt terrible. Guilty. Dirty even. I felt dirty.

GENEVIEVE You're afraid.

GRANDAD I'm bloody scared stiff. I mean, what if she'd said that . . . What if she intimated that I . . . you know, that . . . you know.

GENEVIEVE Look, we can help.

GRANDAD I mean what I could bloody do then. And I can't control her. How do I control her? Can I smack her?

GENEVIEVE No, of course you can't. You can't hit children.

GRANDAD I smacked my kids. I was smacked. It's just what we did. We didn't beat them into submission, we just give 'em a smack. Done. Dealt with. All my dad had to do was rattle the Gazette and we would jump a bloody mile. And now . . . well bloody hell.

I don't know what the rules are any more. What happens when Tit-head comes calling. What do I do then?

GENEVIEVE I'm sorry?

GRANDAD Never mind. And she's gonna be asking questions, wanting to know things, I mean, how can I deal with . . . With all that . . . you know . . . growing up nonsense.

GENEVIEVE She loves you, you know.

GRANDAD She deserves better than me.

GENEVIEVE She thinks the world of you.

GRANDAD I can't do that to her.

GENEVIEVE We can help. Maybe you should just give it a bit more time. A bit more thought.

GRANDAD What the hell do you think I've been doing! I can't get to sleep on a night for bloody thinking about it. Do you think this is easy! It's breaking my bloody heart. I love that little girl more than any bugger else in the world. I could bloody eat her I could. (*A beat.*) How long would it take?

GENEVIEVE Well that, depends.

GRANDAD Can't you give me a straightforward bloody answer?

GENEVIEVE Poppy's old.

GRANDAD She's twelve!

GENEVIEVE And that's why we have to make sure we find her a suitable family. And Poppy would have to like them. They would meet her, with you and then she would go on days out with them, eventually spending a night or a weekend at their house. It could be a while.

GRANDAD And I'll be finished with her.

GENEVIEVE Oh no, no, no, you'd be involved every step of the way and even when she's living with them you could visit and she could visit you. You could be as much a part of her life as you want.

GRANDAD The truth is, I don't know what I bloody want anymore. I need a drink. (*He gets himself a whisky.*) I mean before she came along I was very happy being bloody miserable.

GENEVIEVE Don't make a decision now. You mean more to that little girl than you give yourself credit for. Look, I'll call round in a few days. Give you time to think. But remember, we can help. That's what we're here for.

GRANDAD You keep saying that. You keep saying we can help, we can help. But you only want to help if it fits in with what you want. I live with her. I know her better than anyone. I love her. To you it's a case history. But to me, she is the world. And I want what's best for her. My God I want what's best for her. Genevieve, for God's sake, I am asking you to do this for me. Please. Please.

(*She exits.* GRANDAD *pours himself a whisky. Music in indicates a passage of time.*)

Scene Seven

YOUNG POPPY *bounces in excited. As ever, she absent-mindedly takes a Crunchie from the mantelpiece*

POPPY — Grandad! Grandad! That was the best weekend of my life. We've done loads. We went roller skating. Brian is amazing. *He* can do spins, and jumps. And he's been showing me how to go backwards.

GRANDAD — I know the feeling.

(POPPY *sits in the chair R and starts to play on her phone.*)

POPPY — All my school mates were there, they were dead jealous. Hah. I can't wait to get to school. And we've watched, Pretty Woman and Dirty Dancing. They're Cath's favourite movies. So there. (*She pulls her tongue out at him.*) Oh it was brilliant. And they've got an eighty inch television.

GRANDAD — In the bath?

POPPY — No! In the lounge, it's massive. Eighty inches.

GRANDAD — What are they, gypsies?

POPPY — It's bigger than that one.

GRANDAD — I'd be disappointed if it wasn't.

POPPY — And they said, they would take me to Glastonbury. How amazing is that?

GRANDAD — Yeah, well, we'll see. Go and get ready for bed. (*A beat, he's proud.*) I've done you some Lasagne.

POPPY (*pause*) What?

GRANDAD As a treat.

POPPY You've made me a lasagne.

GRANDAD Yes. (*A beat.*) Jamie Oliver thirty minute recipe. It's taken me four and half hours.

POPPY Oh Grandad that's brilliant. I'll eat it tomorrow.

GRANDAD No, it's ready now, you have to have it while it's hot. Hurry up.

POPPY Oh I couldn't, I'm sorry Grandad, but I've eaten that much this weekend I think I'm gonna burst. Brian is brilliant, he makes everything, oh and his curry, I'm not kidding you, it nearly blew me head off. And we went for an ice-cream and Brian, he's so funny, he said his ice-cream smelt funny, and when Cath smelt it, he shoved it in her face. Oh my God it was hilarious. You should have been there.

GRANDAD (*pause*) Well, get ready for bed then.

POPPY I'll never sleep, ya know. I'm too excited.

GRANDAD And you'll need a bath. There's things to do. You left your bedroom in a right state, you need to get that cleaned up before you get into bed. And you need to put your clothes in the wash and get your school clothes ready, they might need ironing.

POPPY Cath thinks I'm too young to be ironing.

GRANDAD Yeah, but bloody super Cathy isn't here is she and as long as you live under –

POPPY – under my roof you obey my rules.

GRANDAD And you need to do your homework.

POPPY I've done it.

GRANDAD All of it.

POPPY Yeah. *Brian* helped me with it, He doesn't shout or anything, *he's* patient. And oh my God how clever is he?

GRANDAD Let me see it.

POPPY It's in my bag.

GRANDAD Well, get it out then.

POPPY I'll show you later.

GRANDAD I'd like to see it now, if you don't mind.

POPPY I'll show you later.

GRANDAD Right I'll get it myself.

(GRANDAD *advances towards* POPPY'S *bag.*)

POPPY (*a beat*) I'll do it in a minute. God!

GRANDAD (*aggressively and loudly*) Who the hell do you think you're talking to? Don't you ever bloody lie to me, do you hear me or I'll knock your bloody head off.

(POPPY *is noticeably shocked at the violence of the outburst.*)

POPPY Grandad, have you been drinking?

GRANDAD And what if I have. What the hell has that got to do with you? Oh maybe you're going to phone Childline about that an' all are you! Well bloody do it. (*Losing it*). Go on. Go on bloody do it.

POPPY Grandad, stop it.

GRANDAD Use the bloody Bat Phone that Torville and bloody Dean bought you and do it. In fact, I'm going to have another one.

(*He pours himself a whisky and drinks it in one.*)

POPPY What's the matter Grandad?

GRANDAD You! You! You're the matter. You bloody little trouble maker. 'They've got a telly in the bathroom. 'Eighty inches.' What's the matter, is this place not good enough for you?

POPPY No, Grandad!

GRANDAD Now get to bed!

(*She makes her way to the door, stops, thinks and then speaks quietly.*)

POPPY Grandad.

GRANDAD (*aggressively*) Bed! Do you hear me!

(POPPY *squeals and rushes to the door. She stops and turns to see* GRANDAD *with his back turned pouring himself another whisky. She plucks up the courage and gently talks.*)

POPPY They kept calling it my bedroom, and my wardrobe and like, kind of saying things like, 'if you were here more often we could do this and do that' And they were talking about what I would like for Christmas and what we could do for Christmas dinner an' that. You know Grandad, I think they want me to go and live with them.

GRANDAD Good.

(POPPY *starts to get a bit upset.*)

POPPY I won't have to, will I?

GRANDAD You'll do as I bloody say.

POPPY But Grandad –

(GRANDAD *advances towards her, pinning her against the door.*)

GRANDAD You'll go, if I say you're going do you hear me? Do you think this is fun for me? Do you think I enjoy having you here in my house? I'm sick of it do you hear me. I'm sick of it and I'm sick of you! Do you hear me? I'm sick of you. You're a pain in the arse and the sooner you get the hell out of here the better. Now get to bed!

POPPY Please Grandddad. Stop it. I don't like it. I don't like it. I don't like it.

GRANDAD Bed!

(POPPY *opens the door and goes to exit.* GRANDAD *pours another whisky. A long pause. She turns and walks nervously towards him. He turns, she stops. She places the Crunchie on the bed.*)

POPPY I'm sorry about lying about my homework

(*She exits, upset. He flings the Crunchie across the room.*)

GRANDAD Aaaarrggggh!

(*He flops in his chair R. Music in to indicate a passage of time.*)

Scene Eight

Four weeks later. POPPY SENIOR *totters in: she has been drinking.*

POPPY S We need to talk.

GRANDAD I'm going home tomorrow. I need to pack 'cos I'm going home tomorrow.

(YOUNG POPPY *mopes in and flops on the floor, down right.*)

(*to* YOUNG POPPY) What's up with you?

POPPY S What's up with me? What's up with me? I tell you what's up with me.

GRANDAD Come on then.

(POPPY SENIOR *musters up the courage.*)

YOUNG POPPY Somebody said something at school.

POPPY S/ YOUNG POPPY It's about me mam.

Grandad — Come on then spit it out.

Poppy S/
Young Poppy — How did she die?

Grandad — Do I have to go through all this again?

Poppy S/
Young Poppy — Yes, you do.

Grandad — Let's just go and have some tea.

Poppy S/
Young Poppy — Grandad!

Grandad — Alright, alright, calm down. I just don't think it's a good idea dragging all this up, it only upsets you.

Poppy S/
Young Poppy — I want you tell me again, how she died.

Grandad — Let's do this when you get a bit older.

Poppy S — Look at me. (*He looks at her.*) I'm thirty two. (*He looks back at* Young Poppy.)

Grandad — (*confused*) Bloody hell!

Poppy S — (*she sits defiantly, folding her arms*) I'm not moving until you tell me how she died.

Young Poppy — Yesterday, I came out of school and I saw this woman across the street and it looked like me mam. I like called out to her, and she jumped. I like thought she heard me. I was sure it was her. I ran to cross the road but these buses came and when they'd past, she'd gone.

Poppy S — Well!

GRANDAD Okay sweetheart.

POPPY S Sweetheart! Bloody sweetheart!

GRANDAD She'd gone away to London, shopping, as a treat, and she didn't know the roads and a car came from nowhere. She didn't stand a chance. God rest her soul. Her last words before she passed away were 'Tell Poppy, I love her, tell her to be a good girl and tell her to always talk to me, because I will always be there for her.' And then the angels took her.

POPPY S Good God!

YOUNG POPPY Really Grandad?

GRANDAD As God is my judge. She loved you.

POPPY S/ YOUNG POPPY Did she?

GRANDAD She loved you (*All join in.*) all the way to heaven and back.

YOUNG POPPY And I still love her all the way to heaven and back.

(YOUNG POPPY *runs out.*)

POPPY S All the way to heaven and back.

(GRANDAD *is confused and looks after* YOUNG POPPY *who has just exited before looking back at* POPPY S.)

POPPY S She loved me, all the way to heaven and back, well that's amazing because I've just had a letter from her. (GRANDAD *turns to look at her.*) Yes, a letter. I've had a letter from her. Not from heaven funnily enough, but from London. I've had a letter from my mam, from London.

Grandad — Who are you?

Poppy S — Don't start that. I know you know who I am. So don't start playing dumb with me. So 'tell Poppy I love her'. Well she'll be able to tell me herself if I go to London.

Grandad — Who are you?

Poppy S — Don't start playing all Mr Confused with me. My mam's alive isn't she? You've told me that story for years and it's a pack of lies, isn't it?

Grandad — Where's my helper, where's Christine, I need Christine.

Poppy — And the funeral! Oh my God, the funeral! What was all that about? No wonder I couldn't go. I couldn't go because there wasn't one to go to. And the ashes that we scattered at Saltburn. My God! Was everyone in on it: Aunty Margaret, Genevieve? Did everyone go along with your little game? Everybody who I trusted lied to me. Why? Why did you give me all that bullshit?

Grandad — (*calling*) Christine!

Poppy S — If God is your judge, then God help you.

Grandad — Christine!

Poppy S — How could you do that? You can't lie about things like this.

(*He tries to stand.*)

GRANDAD Where's the button?

POPPY S (*sitting him back down*) Oh no you don't.

GRANDAD Press the button.

POPPY S (*raising her voice*) Sit down. You can't lie about things like this. These are people's lives you are messing about with. Who are you, God? You told me she was dead. Why didn't you tell me?

GRANDAD Tell you what!

POPPY S The truth. Why didn't you tell me the truth? I was eleven years old.

GRANDAD I want you to go.

POPPY S I had a right to know. My whole life has been a lie. I have lived a lie, because you didn't have the guts to tell me the truth.

GRANDAD Don't shout at me.

POPPY S I *need* the truth.

GRANDAD (*shouting*) Christine! Christine!

POPPY S And you're gonna remember. Do you hear me? Even if I'm here all night, but you're gonna tell me.

GRANDAD Christine!

POPPY S What happened to me mam?

GRANDAD I don't know.

POPPY S Liar.

GRANDAD I don't know.

POPPY S Why did my mam run away?

GRANDAD I don't know.

POPPY S Liar! Again, why did my mam run away?

GRANDAD I don't know.

POPPY S (*shouting*) Tell me.

GRANDAD I don't know.

POPPY S (*shouting*) Tell me. What happened to me mam?

GRANDAD I don't know. I got a note through the letterbox which said, 'can you pick Poppy up from school, look after her. I'm sorry. I'm so sorry. (*Thinking hard, it starts to come back to him.*) And there was a parcel on the doorstep with all clean clothes and spare uniforms, neatly ironed. (*Pause, he breaks.*) An' I never saw her again.

POPPY S She walked out on me for no reason . . .

GRANDAD I mean she walked out before, when she was young.

POPPY S No.

GRANDAD But she would always turn up again a couple of days later.

POPPY S You're a liar.

GRANDAD Nobody knew where she'd been and she would never talk about it. But this was different. She'd never left a note before. And then the letter came.

POPPY S Letter?

GRANDAD From a kid who'd been paid to deliver it, a couple of days later, apologising and telling me not to look for her.

POPPY S She wouldn't just walk out on me.

GRANDAD Telling me she was finished.

POPPY S She wouldn't do that.

GRANDAD And that I would never find her.

POPPY S My mam loved me.

GRANDAD And I tried.

POPPY S Something must have happened.

GRANDAD Oh God I tried.

POPPY S Because she loved me.

GRANDAD But nothing.

POPPY S She loved me all the way to heaven and back.

GRANDAD She just disappeared.

POPPY S I was her little poppet.

GRANDAD I didn't know what to do.

POPPY S You're a liar.

GRANDAD I did what I thought was best.

POPPY S You're a fucking liar!

GRANDAD She just upped and walked out on her eleven year old daughter.

POPPY S (*screaming*) You're a fucking liar!

(MOLLY *enters.*)

MOLLY Mam, what's up?

POPPY S Wait outside.

GRANDAD (*calling to her*) Poppy! Poppy's here.

MOLLY Why are you shouting?

POPPY S (*raising her voice*) Wait outside.

GRANDAD Poppy, come here darling!

POPPY S (*a final demand*) Molly!

(*MOLLY scarpers outside.*)

GRANDAD Poppy! Where's Poppy gone?

POPPY S You lied to me. You! Of all people! You! I don't know who I am anymore. What have I done that is so bloody awful. Why me? Why did you do it to me? I'm finished with you, do you hear me? Finished with you!

GRANDAD (*with volume*) Good!

POPPY S You twisted, warped old bastard. (*Quiet and full of hatred.*) I hope you rot in hell.

(*She exits. Music to indicate another passage of time. Lights.*)

Scene Nine

MOLLY *walks respectfully into the room.*

MOLLY Grandad.

(GRANDAD'S *face lights up.*)

GRANDAD Poppy!

(*She leans over and kisses him.*)

MOLLY Molly.

GRANDAD What?

MOLLY I'm Molly, Poppy is my mam.

GRANDAD Molly is my wife. You're Poppy.

MOLLY I'm your granddaughter, Molly.

GRANDAD Molly's my wife.

MOLLY Grandad. I'm your great granddaughter, Molly, I'm Poppy's daughter.

GRANDAD She's only twelve.

MOLLY That's how old I am.

GRANDAD You're the same age as your mam.

MOLLY I'm just going a bit mad, Grandad.

GRANDAD You wanna get that looked at.

MOLLY	How are you Grandad?
GRANDAD	Well, I feel a lot better 'cos I'm going home tomorrow.
MOLLY	What?
GRANDAD	Can you ring home and tell Molly I'm sorry for being late?
MOLLY	I haven't got a phone.
GRANDAD	(*shocked*) You haven't got a phone!
MOLLY	Me mam won't let me have one until I'm fourteen.
GRANDAD	Good God!
MOLLY	She said it's bad for me.
GRANDAD	How do you get in touch with your friends?
MOLLY	Tell me about it.
GRANDAD	You can't not have a phone.
MOLLY	I miss out on loads of things that get arranged at the last minute.
GRANDAD	What about your computer?
MOLLY	I can only go on to it an hour a night, unless I need it for homework.
GRANDAD	This is abuse.
MOLLY	I know.
GRANDAD	What the hell do you do all the time?

MOLLY Homework! Dancing, singing lessons, gym.

GRANDAD You need to tell her. What do they call her this mother of yours?

MOLLY Poppy.

GRANDAD I have a granddaughter called Poppy. What a small world. (*A sudden thought.*) Hey, I've got a phone you can have.

MOLLY But me mam –

GRANDAD Bugger your mam. You can't not have a phone. It's over there.

MOLLY I don't think –

GRANDAD For God's sake get some backbone. Where's your fight. You need to stick up for yourself.

MOLLY Grandad, I'm only twelve.

GRANDAD Yeah. Almost a woman. I've got all my music on me phone.

MOLLY You haven't!

GRANDAD I went to College. I am a Silver surfer. I can go on my phone press a few buttons and get any music I like. Go on then get it, it's over there.

MOLLY But I'll get in to trouble.

GRANDAD Leave your bloody mother to me. What do they call her?

MOLLY (*pause*) Pam.

Grandad (*waving her over*) Go on then.

Molly What is this?

Grandad It's a phone.

Molly Yeah but like how old is it.

Grandad It's never been used.

Molly I don't care. I don't want this.

Grandad What's wrong with it?

Molly Look at it. It's like ancient. I don't even think I could work it.

Grandad Have you got a phone?

Molly No.

Grandad Well bloody take it and stop complaining.

(Poppy S *enters,* Molly *quickly hides the phone.*)

Poppy S Okay darling, say goodbye to your Grandad.

Molly 'Bye Grandad.

(*She gives him a kiss.*)

Grandad 'Bye Poppy.

(Molly *makes her way to the door.*)

Poppy S Now you know what you promised me.

Molly Yes.

(MOLLY *exits.* POPPY S *is much calmer. Gone is the fiery exchange of earlier. Things are much more reasoned.*)

GRANDAD Have you come to take me home?

POPPY S Rose. Do you want to meet her?

GRANDAD Molly will wonder where the hell I am.

POPPY S She wants to know if you'll see her.

GRANDAD I've been out for hours.

POPPY S Are you listening to me? Rose wants to meet up with you.

GRANDAD Rose?

POPPY S Yes. Rose. Rose is alive.

GRANDAD Rose?

POPPY S Yes. Rose, your daughter. She wants to meet you. Do *you* want to meet her? (*Pause.*) Do you want to see her?

GRANDAD (*pause*) Baby Rose?

POPPY S She wants to meet me. (*He looks at her.*) I keep asking myself, what could she say to me that would make me feel better. And I don't think there's anything. Why now? It doesn't make sense. You know I look at my little girl and see her face and watch her smile and for the life of me I don't know how anybody can do what Rose did to me.

GRANDAD Molly will sort her out. One word from Molly . . . ooh and Rose will be right in the doghouse.

POPPY S — I went to see to my mam. Cath. (*Pause.*) She's told me about you.

GRANDAD — She'll apologise. Molly will make sure of that.

POPPY S — You kept in touch with Cath, didn't you?

GRANDAD — I'll see Molly tomorrow, when I get home.

POPPY S — You spoke to her regularly. You even went to the house before I did, to suss it out.

GRANDAD — She'll be wondering where I am.

POPPY S — You knew where they lived and you let me go on lying about what a mansion it was. Tellys in the bathroom and all that rubbish. You knew they didn't have two halfpennies to rub together, didn't you? And you let me go on and on about how much they had. And you paid for everything! (*A beat.*) So why didn't you come and visit me? Grandad, look at me. Look at me. (*He looks at her.*) When I was little, why didn't you come and visit me?

GRANDAD — Visit you? You're here aren't you?

POPPY S — You promised when I went to Cath and Brian's you said that you would visit me and you didn't. Why didn't you? Why didn't you answer my calls, me letters? You know all I ever wanted was to watch the cricket and have a bloody good argument. I cried myself to sleep when we moved down South, because I knew that I would never see you. I thought you hated me. If Aunty Margaret hadn't got in touch last year, I might never have seen you again. Why didn't you visit me?

Grandad — Who?

Poppy S — Me. Why didn't you visit me, Poppy when I was a little girl?

Grandad — Poppy?

Poppy S — Yes Poppy. Poppy. You knew she was desperate for you. So why didn't you visit Poppy when she was a little girl.

(*A long silence.*)

Grandad — I did go round – a couple of times.

Poppy S — But you stopped.

Grandad — I couldn't do it. Poppy was mine, not theirs. I was jealous. I said things. I had a temper. There were fights. I knew what she needed, not them.

Poppy S — Then why get rid of her? If she meant that much to you why not bring her up? Why not fight to keep her?

Grandad — I was old.

Poppy S — She wanted to stay with you. .

Grandad — I was no good for her.

Poppy S — You don't know how much she wanted you.

Grandad — I wasn't the man she thought I was.

Poppy S — You were.

GRANDAD No, I was a bully.

POPPY S But you were her Grandad and she loved you. She loved you more than you'll ever know.

GRANDAD Did she?

POPPY S Yes. Yes she did.

GRANDAD (*smiles*) Poppy loved me!

(POPPY S *kneels at his feet and takes his hand.*)

POPPY S Poppy loved you very much.

GRANDAD (*smiles*) I would give anything to see her again. Just for a couple of minutes. Just to have a little chat with her. (*Becomes upset.*) Just to tell her, I'm sorry. I let her down didn't I? She was the best thing that ever happened to me. What a lassie she was.

POPPY S Every time I've done anything, it's always been, what will my Grandad think? Would he approve? Will I be good enough for my Grandad? When I'm talking to Molly – *my daughter* – I can hear you talking. 'Manners don't cost anything', 'Cleanliness is next to Godliness', 'Door'.

(*Pause.* GRANDAD *takes her hand.*)

GRANDAD Would you like do a jigsaw?

POPPY S What?

GRANDAD Would you like to do a jigsaw?

POPPY S (*pause, she smiles*) I would absolutely love to do a jigsaw.

(POPPY S *makes her way to fetch the jigsaw that was placed U.S. of the bed and places it on the small table that goes over the bed.* GRANDAD *makes his way to the bed.*)

GRANDAD (*happy*) Oh great. There's a new one over there. Go and get it. Christine got me it. She's nice, Christine. She looks after me; I'll miss her when I go home. It's a good un an' all. I've already started it. It's difficult. Look at all that sky. You always have to find the corners first.

POPPY S And the end pieces.

GRANDAD (*surprised*) You've done one before?

POPPY S I used to do them with my Grandad.

GRANDAD I used to do them with our Poppy.

(*They are both sat on the bed with the jigsaw on the table in front of them.*)

POPPY S *Our* Poppy.

GRANDAD Do you know her?

POPPY S Yes, yes I know her.

GRANDAD She was a good singer.

POPPY S She was the best.

GRANDAD She could have been somebody.

POPPY S I think she is somebody.

GRANDAD I used to love to hear her sing. She sang at Blackpool.

POPPY S I was there.

GRANDAD Were you?

POPPY S Yeah.

GRANDAD How good was she! I've got another bit.

POPPY S Were you there, because I thought I saw you.

GRANDAD (*sings*) *Hey look me over, lend me an ear.* That's what she sang.

POPPY S I can remember it.

GRANDAD I can then.

POPPY S I'll never forget it.

GRANDAD Nor me. She was a little beauty.

POPPY S I've got the final side piece. All corners and sides are done.

GRANDAD Now, start with the sky. It's always best to start with the sky.

(*Lights and blackout.*)